ULTIMATE
OWNER'S GUIDE

Porsche 911 (996)

GW00383157

Richard Hamilton
PMM Books

The information presented here represents the best available to the author at the time of going to press. The book is intended as a guide only. The author, the publisher or the associated companies can accept no liabilities for any material loss resulting from the use of this information.

This book uses model names, type numbers and terms that are the property of the trademark holders and are used here for identification only. Several specialists or specific brands are mentioned throughout the book. These are products and services that have only been spoken of positively by the experts who have contributed to this book. These specialists have made no commercial endorsement to the author or publisher.

This is an independent publication.
There is no association with Porsche SE or any of its subsidiaries. The name of Porsche is used only for identification purposes.

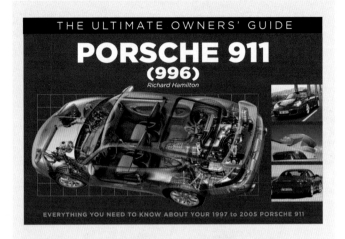

THE ULTIMATE OWNERS' GUIDE

PORSCHE 911
(996)
Richard Hamilton

EVERYTHING YOU NEED TO KNOW ABOUT YOUR 1997 to 2005 PORSCHE 911

Copyright: Richard Hamilton 2012

First published 2012.   ISBN 978 1 906712 03 7

Design & Layout: SD Design

Photo credits: Richard Hamilton, Min Chew, Porsche Archive

Published by PMM Books, an imprint of Peter Morgan Media Ltd., PO Box 2561, Marlborough, Wiltshire, SN8 1YD, Great Britain.
Telephone: +44 1672 514038 **E-mail:** sales@pmmbooks.com **Website:** www.pmmbooks.com

Contents

Introduction

So how did you arrive at a 996? Most people answer "I've wanted a 911 since I was a teenager". Well, I will come straight out and admit it. It was a picture of a Ferrari 246 Dino on my bedroom wall in my late teens, not a Porsche 930 Turbo! Alongside it was a Maserati 250F Grand Prix car, driven by my childhood hero Juan Fangio – so that might give you an idea of my age and early taste in cars!

The other popular reason given for wanting to own a 911 is simply as a progression from another Porsche model.

The 911 appeals to all enthusiasts

That is how it was for me. After starting out with a 1994 993, I moved to a 1998 Carrera 2, and on to my current 2000 996 Turbo.

The 911 appeals to enthusiasts of all ages, but for most of us the attraction is owning a small part of Porsche's heritage and engineering pedigree.

Early 996s are now well over 10 years old and due to the much higher volume production than earlier 911s, are becoming affordable to a much wider audience. Although the engine is in the same place, they are radically different to earlier models with the original design being brought into the modern era. This makes them very much more friendly for day-to-day use, and hence a more practical daily driver for more people than before.

This affordability brings with it its own problems. A 10 year old car requires more maintenance in order to keep it in tip-top condition and this can be an expensive exercise. All too often cars find themselves on the market after having been neglected by previous owners who could not afford the maintenance – so buy carefully.

This book is intended to help the

A 1998 pre-facelift model (996.1)

'Facelift' (996.2) Cabrio in Speed Yellow

owner with some basic home mechanic
skills to get the most from their car. It
covers some basic procedures, but it's
very important to say that you should
never attempt any operations unless you
feel both able and comfortable about
completing the task without danger to
yourself or the vehicle. Always work
safely, and use good quality tools. Bear
in mind that if you have an extended
Porsche warranty it may be affected by
the use of aftermarket items. 996

Richard Hamilton
Maidenhead, England

*The author's two 911s,
a 2000 Turbo Coupé and
1989 3.2 Carrera Sport*

I f you are new to the brand, you may find the many abbreviations and acronyms used by the dealer or on forums bewildering. Here are some of the most popular with a brief description. Many of these will be detailed later in the book.

ABD *Automatic Brake Differential* – the system of braking individual rear wheels as part of the traction control system.

ABS *Anti-lock Brake System* – a system to prevent locking of the wheels under braking to maintain control.

AOS *Air/Oil Separator* – a device which separates oil mist from the crankcase fumes which are recycled into the inlet manifold as part of emissions control.

ASR *Anti-Slip Regulation* – the reduction of torque to the rear wheels as part of the traction control system.

CAN *Controller Area Network* – a two-wire communication system between various control modules of the car.

DME *Digitale Motor Elektronik* - the engine's electronic control unit.

DSP *Digital Sound Processing* – an optional audio enhancement.

IMS *Intermediate Shaft* – the drive shaft which connects the crankshaft to the camshaft timing chain drive. IMS is also commonly used when describing the seal of its support bearing at the flywheel end.

Carrera Cabriolet

IPAS *Integrated Porsche trader Access Program* – The Porsche security codes database.

MAF *Mass Air Flow (sensor)* – measures the air flow into the engine.

MOST *Media Oriented Systems Transport* – the fibre optic communication ring connecting elements of the audio system.

MY *Model Year* – Porsche model years start on 1st September, so a car produced on, say, 1st October 1999 will be a MY2000 car.

OBD *On Board Diagnosis* – The system of connecting the car to a computer for diagnostic purposes.

OPC *Official Porsche Centre*, sometimes referred to as simply PCs.

PCCB *Porsche Ceramic Composite Brakes* – the optional ceramic disk (rotor) brake system which provides much enhanced braking ability.

PCM *Porsche Communications Management* – an audio system of radio, CD, and satellite navigation, with optional telephone, amplifier, and CD changer.

PET *Porsche Elektronischer Teilekatalog* – the Porsche electronic parts catalogue.

PIWIS *Porsche Integrated Workshop Information System* – the latest Porsche diagnostic computer.

POSIP *Porsche Side Impact Protection System* – side airbag system (in doors).

PSE *Porsche Sports Exhaust* - a sports exhaust system which is switchable between normal and loud modes.

PST 2 *Porsche System Tester 2* – predecessor to PIWIS.

PSM *Porsche Stability Management* – a system that controls braking of individual wheels, and engine power regulation, to maximise traction and stability.

PU *PolyUrethane* – commonly used to describe the front and rear bumpers, derived from the generic term for the material from which they are manufactured.

RMS *Rear Main (oil) Seal* – the crankshaft seal at the flywheel end of the engine.

RoW *Rest of the World* – in Porsche terms, usually everywhere except USA/Canada.

TC *Traction Control* – a system for preventing wheelspin.

TSB *Technical Service Bulletin* – Porsche bulletins covering updates and modifications.

VIL *Vehicle Identification Label* – the label in the Maintenance Booklet and on the underside of the front luggage compartment showing various vehicle build information.

VIN *Vehicle Identification Number* – the unique 17-digit identification number. *996*

Metric/Imperial/US Units

Here are some common conversions from Metric to the Imperial and US systems:

To convert:
millimetres to inches
divide by 25.4 (1000mm=1 metre)

kilograms to pounds
multiply by 2.205

litres to imperial gallons
multiply by 0.212

litres to US gallons
multiply by 0.264

Imperial gallons to US gallons
multiply by 1.201

kilometres to miles
multiply by 0.621

Newton-metres (Nm) to pound-force foot (lbf-ft)
multiply by 0.738

°C to °F
multiply by 1.8 and add 32

Evolution

Design studio in Weissach. At the rear Lai and Lagaay discuss their new creation

By the mid-1990s, 911 production costs had reached an unsustainable level, and something had to give. The 993 design was the final development of the 911, which had been around for over 30 years. Albeit a wonderful machine, a complete redesign was needed for Porsche to survive.

With its new appearance overseen by head of Porsche Styling, Harm Lagaay and body styling the work of Pinky Lai, the 996 Carrera was new from the ground up – bigger, stiffer, lighter, more powerful and with a more spacious, luxurious interior. However, it remained instantly recognisable as a 911.

The front end, from the front bumper to the windshield, was virtually identical to the recently introduced 986 Boxster model, but the cabin area followed the classic 911 4-seat configuration with the engine overhanging the rear axle. 30mm (1.18 inches) wider and 173mm (6.81 inches) longer than its predecessor, the structural stiffness of the new bodyshell was up by 45% in torsion and 50% in flexure. Drag coefficient was down to 0.3 from 0.33. The car was also much cheaper to produce than the 993 – the result of bringing in Japanese consultants to assist with production design and manufacturing techniques.

The suspension used a MacPherson strut design at the front and a cast aluminium multi-link design at the rear. The longer wheelbase and more rigid structure proved to be an excellent platform for the new suspension arrangement.

The biggest departure from Porsche convention or the new 911 was the introduction of water cooling for the 3.4 litre, flat-6 engine. This was an almost unavoidable necessity to meet new exhaust emissions and noise regulations. The same basic design as the Boxster, (which began life at 2.5-litres), the engine used 4-valve technology with a new Variocam variable valve timing system for adjusting the camshaft timing. This resulted in an increase in torque and a reduction of hydrocarbon emissions. The engine also featured what can only be described as a 'semi-wet' sump, as the oil reservoir was incorporated within the crankcase.

Transmission was provided by either a manual 6-speed transmission manufactured by Getrag or a 5-speed Tiptronic S automatic gearbox supplied by ZF.

On the inside the transformation was also extensive. Gone was the seemingly haphazard arrangement of switchgear and instruments, which had been carried over from previous models all the way to the

993. A much more practical and ergonomic layout took its place that retained some of the signature Porsche 911 features, including the large central rev-counter. The driving position was also improved with wider spaced pedals that were more centrally mounted in the footwell. Water cooling also had the big advantage in providing a far superior heating system and true climate control was introduced using a system from Audi. The cabin was a much more refined place to be than ever before.

The car had its world debut at the Frankfurt Motor show in September 1997 and went on sale immediately in Europe in conventional rear-wheel drive form. It was an instant success and the more modern design attracted many new non-traditional Porsche buyers. Although 14 cars were built in Model Year 1997 (presumably pre-production and press cars), volume sales began in MY1998 (starting September 1997) in Europe and MY1999 (starting August 1998 in the USA). Over the following seven years, several new variants were introduced and these are outlined in the following tables. 996

The 996 (in red) was much cheaper to build than the previous 993

MY2005 Turbo S,
the last of the line

MY1998

The Carrera 2 was introduced for the 1998 model year at the Frankfurt auto show in September 1997. It was powered by an all-new 3387cc flat-6, 24-valve water-cooled engine with variable valve timing, producing 300hp (220kW). Transmissions were a choice of a 6-speed manual gearbox made by Getrag or a 5-speed automatic Tiptronic gearbox made by ZF. Standard fitment were 17-inch alloy wheels, ABS, radio-cassette and remote alarm system. There was also a substantial array of optional extras to choose from.

The Coupé version was joined by the Cabriolet in the summer of 1998.

MY1999

The Cabriolet and 4-wheel-drive Carrera 4 versions of the 996 were unveiled at the Paris auto show in October 1998, for the 1999 model year. New features included the Porsche Side Impact Protection System (POSIP) and clear turn signal lenses front and rear, to distinguish the car from the Boxster

MY1998 Carrera 2 Coupé

and to counter negative criticism of the 'fried egg' look of the front lights. The Cabriolet was around 10% more to purchase than the Coupé equivalent, but the roof mechanism was fast, and could lower or raise in just 20 seconds. A removable hardtop was also a standard feature of the Cabriolet, colour-coded to the bodywork.

The 4-wheel drive system was available

for both Coupé and Cabriolet and cost nearly 7% more than the 2-wheel drive model. Various modifications to the front end were required to make room for the front axle final drive, which resulted in a smaller front luggage compartment, and the use of a deflated space-saver wheel under the floor of the compartment. The C4 was also available in Tiptronic transmission for the first time. Engine management was by the Bosch Motronic 7.2 DME, which introduced drive-by-wire throttle control, often referred to as eGas.

The 4-wheel drive system added 55kg (121lbs) to the overall weight, but performance figures were quoted identical to the C2 equivalent due to improved traction. The extra weight at the front end gave a weight balance of 40-60%, compared with 38-62% for the C2. The 4-piston calipers manufactured for Porsche by Brembo were painted in a 'titanium' (silver) colour for the C4, as opposed to black for the C2. Perhaps the most significant introduction on the C4 was Porsche Stability Management (PSM). To quote the Porsche Service Information Document of the time: "PSM is an active control system for stabilising a vehicle at the limit of its driving dynamics capability. PSM includes functions such as ABS, ABD, ASR (traction-slip control), EBV (Electronic Brake-force Distribution), as well as longitudinal dynamics control with MSR (engine drag torque control). In addition to this, the vehicle is stabilised at the limit of its driving dynamics capability

within the transverse dynamics control system by FDR (driving dynamics control).

From the outside there is virtually no difference in appearance, other than the Carrera 4 engine compartment badge, silver calipers, and a new design of 17-inch alloy wheels.

MY2000

Changes for Model Year 2000 included the adoption of Motronic 7.2 (eGas) to all Carrera models, and the option of PSM on C2 models, which had previously been offered with a basic traction control system based on ABS 5.3.

MY1999 Cabriolet

Production numbers

Model Year	C2 Cpe.	C2 Cab.	C4 Cpe.	C4 Cab.	4S Cpe.	4S Cab.	Targa	Turbo Cpe.	
MY1997 (V)	14								
MY1998 (W)	8296	952							
MY1999 (X)	10728	9458	4773	3081					
MY2000 (Y)	6107	6743	3862	2828				16	
MY2001 (1)	6543	6721	4085	3655	15		63	5324	
MY2002 (2)	6249	6978	1722	3870	4802		2630	5908	
MY2003 (3)	4987	4973	1147	2930	7388	451	1812	4322	
MY2004 (4)	3393	2809	362	355	4365	4543	508	1273	
MY2005 (5)		201			728	763	129	122	
Totals	46317	38835	15951	16719	17298	5757	5142	16965	

MY2000 GT3 at Porsche's Zuffenhausen, Stuttgart offices.
Note the unusual graphics

Although it was released in May 1999, the new GT3 was designated MY2000 and issued chassis numbers accordingly. This was a far more track-focussed machine than the regular Carrera, effectively taking the place of the older Carrera RS models.

It was powered by a new 3600cc engine based on the crankcase of the Le Mans-winning GT1 engine, with new water-cooled cylinder blocks. 3600cc capacity with 4 valves per cylinder, it retained the Motronic 5.2.2 DME of the

Turbo Cab.	Turbo S Cpe.	Turbo S Cab.	GT2	GT3	GT3RS	GT3R (M005)	Cup (M001)	Total
								14
								9248
								28040
				1360		63		20979
			247	508			114	27275
			716				138	33013
308			233	781	4		200	29536
3099	2	3	73	1532	678		150	23145
127	598	960	18	276			90	4012
3534	**600**	**963**	**1287**	**4457**	**682**	**63**	**692**	**175262**

earlier Carreras and had an output of 360bhp (265kW).

With the rear wheels only driven, the GT3 used the stiffer C4 bodyshell. The suspension was lowered by 30mm (1.18 inches), with stiffer springs and anti-roll (sway) bars, adjustable ride height and reinforced mounting points. The brakes were upgraded to match the increased power and weight was reduced by the removal of sound deadening material and the rear seats.

Also released for MY2000 was the special Millennium Edition.

Based on the Carrera 4, the production run was limited to 911 examples. The cars were presented in a special Violet Chromaflair paintwork and highly polished 18" Turbo Look 1 wheels. The engine was the standard 3.4-litre unit and transmissions were the 6-speed manual or 5-speed Tiptronic gearboxes. Suspension was the M030 sports package.

However, it was the opulent interior that set the car apart, with it's Natural leather, and burr wood trim. It had just

about every conceivable extra fitted as standard, including cruise control, on-board computer, PCM1 and telephone, to name a few.

The summer of 2000 also saw the long-awaited introduction of the new 996 Turbo (with all cars having a MY2001 VIN). Like the GT3, the engine was based on the Le Mans-winning GT1 crankcase. With new water cooled cylinder blocks, 3600cc capacity and 4 valves per cylinder, it featured the new Variocam Plus system of variable valve

Model Year 1998

996 Carrera 2 Coupé introduced

3387cc, 6-cylinder, 300hp (220kW) engine

6-speed manual or 5-speed ZF Tiptronic gearbox

Bosch Motronic 5.2.2 DME (mechanical throttle)

17-inch wheels

Numerous options including:

18-inch wheels

Sports suspension

Traction control

Climate control air conditioning

Cruise control

On-board computer

Sports exhaust

Carrera 2 Cabriolet introduced Summer 1998

Specifications generally as above

Model Year 1999

996 Carrera 4 Coupé & Cabriolet introduced

3387cc, 6-cylinder, 300hp (220kW) engine

6-speed manual or 5-speed ZF Tiptronic gearbox

with Bosch Motronic 7.2 (electronic throttle)

PSM introduced on C4

POSIP introduced

Clear indicator lenses introduced

Model Year 2000

Bosch Motronic 7.2 DME now fitted to C2 models

PSM now optional on C2 models

Special "Millennium" Edition

3387cc, 6-cylinder, 300hp (220kW) engine

6-speed manual or 5-speed ZF Tiptronic gearbox

996 GT3 introduced

3600cc, 6-cylinder, 360hp (265kW) engine

6-speed manual gearbox

Model Year 2001

Electric operation of luggage and engine lids

996 Turbo Coupé introduced (car released in Summer 2000 with MY2001 VIN)

3600cc, 6-cylinder, twin-turbo 420hp (310kW) engine

6-speed manual or 5-speed MB Tiptronic gearbox

Bosch Motronic 7.8 DME

996 GT2 introduced

3600cc, 6-cylinder, twin-turbo 462hp (340kW) engine

6-speed manual gearbox

MY2000 Millennium Edition

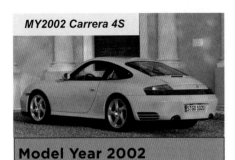
MY2002 Carrera 4S

Model Year 2002

Facelift Carrera models introduced.

3596cc, 6-cylinder, 320hp (235kW) engine

6-speed manual or 5-speed MB Tiptronic gearbox

Bosch Motronic 7.8 DME

Options similar to MY1999

Heated glass rear window on Cabriolet

Targa introduced (2wd only)

3596cc, 6-cylinder, 320hp (235kW) engine

6-speed manual or 5-speed MB Tiptronic gearbox

C4S Coupé introduced

3596cc, 6-cylinder, 320hp (235kW)engine

6-speed manual or 5-speed MB Tiptronic gearbox

X50 Power Kit option introduced on Turbo

Model Year 2003

MOST communication bus introduced

PCM2.0 introduced

C4S Cabriolet introduced

3596cc, 6-cylinder, 320hp (235kW) engine

6-speed manual or 5-speed MB Tiptronic gearbox

Turbo Cabriolet introduced

3600cc, 6-cylinder, twin-turbo 420hp (310kW) engine

6-speed manual or 5-speed MB Tiptronic gearbox

Facelift GT3 introduced with uprated 381hp (280kW) engine

6-speed manual gearbox only

MY2003 GT3

Model Year 2004

Special "Anniversary" Edition

3596cc, 6-cylinder, 345hp (254kW) engine (X50)

6-speed manual or 5-speed MB Tiptronic gearbox

GT3 RS introduced

3600cc, 6-cylinder, 381hp (280kW) engine

6-speed manual gearbox

Model Year 2005

996 Turbo S and Turbo S Cabriolet introduced

3600cc, 6-cylinder, twin-turbo 450hp (342kW) engine

6-speed manual or 5-speed MB Tiptronic gearbox

C2 Coupé and C4 Coupé and Cabriolet discontinued

All 996 production discontinued in MY2006

timing and lift. It was equipped with two K16 turbochargers and had an output of 420hp (310kW) at 6000rpm.

The Turbo had new front fenders and headlights and 60mm (2.36 inches) wider bodywork at the rear, with distinctive intercooler air inlets in the rear wings. Sitting on 10mm (0.4 inch) lower sports suspension and uprated brakes and shock absorbers, it used the all-wheel drive system from the Carrera 4. Transmission was either a 6-speed manual gearbox, or a Mercedes Benz derived Tiptronic automatic 5-speed gearbox.

The Turbo was an instant hit and created a long waiting list of purchasers.

MY2001

New for MY2001 was the introduction of the most powerful 996 to date – the extreme GT2. The engine was an uprated 3600cc Turbo unit, with larger K24 turbochargers, producing 462hp (340kW) at 5700rpm.

The body was from the Turbo, but the GT2 was only available with manual transmission and rear wheel drive. With

no option of Traction Control available, it made for an extremely exciting drive, even with the 12-inch wide rear rims.

A Clubsport version of the GT2 was also available, with a bolt-in roll cage, racing bucket seats, 6-point racing harness, fire extinguisher and battery kill switch. This was definitely not for the faint-hearted!

The only minor change for the MY2001 Carrera models was the change to electrically operated luggage and engine compartment lids.

MY2002

The Frankfurt Motor Show in September 2001 bought the most significant changes to the 996. In addition to a more powerful

MY2002 saw the most significant changes to the 996 family

3.6 litre engine and styling changes to the existing model range, there were two new models – the C4S and Targa.

Visually, the main change to the Carrera 2 and 4 was to the front and rear bumpers, with the fenders incorporating the headlight assemblies from the Turbo. The front and rear bumpers were also modified to give a 'skirt' effect around the bottom edges, giving them a slightly more aggressive appearance. Overall, this gave the Carreras a noticeably different front-end look to the Boxster, as it was a common criticism that they looked too similar.

Engine capacity was enlarged from 3387cc to 3596cc and there was a resulting power increase from 300hp (220kW) to 320hp (235kW) at 6800rpm. Engine management changed to the Bosch Motronic 7.8 system. The Variocam Plus system, first used on the Turbo, was also introduced along with larger valves. The package resulted in improved fuel economy. The new exhaust system was optimised for sound, within permissible noise limit values.

Both manual and Tiptronic transmissions were strengthened accordingly. The 6-speed gearbox had an extra bearing on the input shaft, while the Tiptronic was completely revised, now being based on the (Mercedes derived) Turbo unit. Inside the cabin there were several subtle changes. A glovebox and integrated cupholders brought convenience to the front seat passengers.

The revised instrument cluster had a far more comprehensive on-board computer system. Control buttons were flat (rather than gloss) finished to give a perceived improvement of quality, while a three-spoke steering wheel became standard. Other minor improvements included seat belt tensioners with belt force limiters and a larger centre air conditioning vent. The memory seat option now included memory via the key fob. On a technical level, CAN wiring of the instrument cluster, DME, Tiptronic, PSM and air conditioning was introduced.

There were some improvements to the 996's running gear. The front track was widened by 10mm (0.4in). Standard

MY2002 Targa

17-inch wheels remained at 7-inch (F) and 9-inch(R) wide, but the optional 18-inch alloys became 8-inch and 10-inches wide respectively. Extensive reinforcement of the roof frame, sills and seat pan area increased stiffness of the Coupé by 25% and by 10% for the Cabriolet.

A very welcome and significant improvement for the 2002 Cabriolet was the introduction of a heated glass rear window. In addition, the rear window was made as part of a detachable panel, so that if either the roof fabric or the glass window were to be damaged, they could be changed independently.

The new Targa followed the concept introduced on the 993. A large, electrically controlled, glass roof panel slid back under the rear window to give open top motoring. When closed it gave the security and closed-cockpit sensation of a Coupé. When the roof was closed the rear window could be opened like a hatchback tailgate to allow luggage to be loaded into the rear of the car. An electrically operated blind covered the underside of the glass roof to give protection from the sun with the roof closed, if required. The glass roof gave a light and airy feel to the interior.

The Targa was only available in rear wheel drive and weighed a full 80kg (176lb) more than the Coupé. As a result, Porsche quoted 0-62mph times comparable to those of the Cabriolet. The car was also fitted with stiffer anti-roll (sway) bars, as the centre of gravity was higher. The modified roofline gave the Targa slightly more headroom and a little more luggage space behind the rear seats, compared to the Coupé.

The new Carrera 4S used the wide body of the Turbo, but without the

Turbo's rear spoiler or air inlet scoops in the rear fenders. It also featured a red rear reflector strip between the lights, reminiscent of earlier 911s. The C4S suspension and brakes was based on the Turbo's, including the attractive Turbo Look II 18-inch alloys, and ran a 10mm (0.4 inch) lower ride height compared to the regular Carrera.

Regarded as the best looking 996 type,it is probably the most sought after Carrera model on the used car market.

MY2003

Summer 2003 saw the introduction of the C4S and Turbo Cabriolet models. A feature of all the 2003 Cabriolets was that the roof could now be raised and lowered at speeds of up to 30mph. A new GPS satellite navigation system – Porsche Communications Management (PCM) 2.0 – was also introduced in 2003, along with the MOST fibre-optic audio communication system.

2003 also saw the introduction of the new facelift GT3. Available in Comfort, or with a no-cost optional Clubsport package,

the engine output was raised to 381hp (280kW) at 7400rpm. It sat 20mm (0.79 inch) lower than the regular Carreras and had larger (350mm (13.8in) F & 330mm (13in) R) brake discs (rotors) and 6-piston monobloc (single piece) front calipers.

Porsche Ceramic Composite Brakes (PCCB) were an option to further enhance the stopping power.

The GT3 had a distinctive new fixed rear wing and 10-spoke alloy wheels. Other improvements were the addition of a gearbox oil cooler and steel synchromesh rings in the gearbox

The GT2 engine was uprated even further for 2003, now delivering a mighty 483hp (365kW) and pushing the top speed to just under 200mph.

MY2004

In September 2003, the Carrera Anniversary was a limited edition model to celebrate 40 years of the 911. Finished in special 'GT silver' metallic paint, it featured turbo front grilles, chrome 18-inch alloys and chrome tailpipes. The engine produced 345hp (254kW), thanks

to the X51 powerkit that lifted maximum power by 25hp (16kW) over the standard Carreras. The suspension was the M030 Sports type – stiffened and lowered by 10mm (0.4 inch).

The cabin featured Natural dark grey leather and various items of body coloured trim. Only 1963 examples were produced and each is uniquely badged with the '911' script on the engine compartment lid.

For MY2004 only, Porsche announced their ultimate track day weapon – the uncompromising GT3 RS.

Essentially an homologation special to meet FIA N-GT rules, weight saving was the order of the day. The front

MY2005 Turbo S Cabriolet

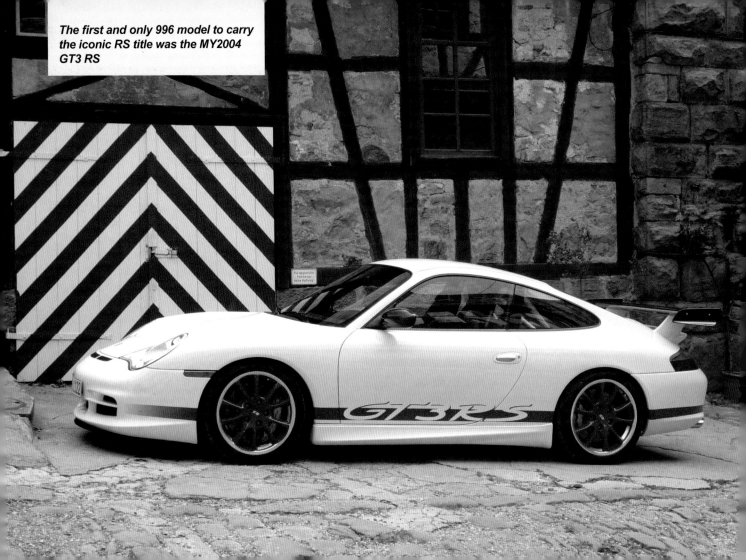

The first and only 996 model to carry the iconic RS title was the MY2004 GT3 RS

compartment lid was made from carbon fibre reinforced plastic, as was the large rear wing, and the rear screen was also made from a clear polycarbonate material. Inside, lightweight bucket seats and the removal of items such as audio equipment also helped to shed the pounds. Despite the heavy, full rollover cage it was 20kg (44lb) less than the standard GT3. Air conditioning and in-car entertainment were optional equipment.

All the cars were finished in Carrara White paintwork, with a choice of red or blue decals and wheels.

MY2005

Production of the C2 Coupé, C4 Coupé and C4 Cabriolet ceased at the end of MY2004, after the introduction of the 997 for MY2005. The other 996 models continued in production, but in smaller numbers, to fill the gaps in the new 997 range.

However, Porsche were not finished with the 996 and released their end-of-the-line tribute to the 996 model – the Turbo S.

The MY2004 Anniversary Edition's appeal was lifted by the X51 powerkit

The 'S' was offered in Coupé and Cabriolet versions, both powered by the X50 version of the twin-turbocharged engine, having an output of 450hp (330kW) at 5700rpm. Stopping power was provided by PCCBs and the interior was finished with a host of goodies as standard, including PCM with GPS navigation, a CD autochanger, cruise control and aluminium faced dials.

Outside, a special colour option of Dark Olive metallic was offered and the 18-inch alloys were finished in GT Silver metallic.

All in all, a fine end to a seven year production run! `996`

You now have your new-to-you 996. No doubt your primary criteria when choosing it were model, colour and interior. You may also have had some other 'tick boxes' such as wheel preference, navigation or sports exhaust, but undoubtedly the car will have other options fitted. The 996 option list is extensive, to say the least, allowing the original purchaser to tailor the car to his or her requirements, and budget of course.

So where do you find out exactly what you have? The primary source of this information is the Vehicle Identification Label. When the car was produced, two of these labels were supplied, and fitted by the dealer. One is attached to the underside of the luggage compartment lid (up to MY2005) and the other is in the front of the Guarantee and Maintenance Booklet.

A useful VIN decoder can be found at www.renntech.org.

The VIL shows:

(1) Vehicle Identification Number
(2) Vehicle Order Code
(3) Engine Code
(4) Transmission Code
(5) Paint Code
(6) Interior Trim Code
(7) Country and Option Codes

(1) WP0ZZZ99z1S000000
(2) 996 421
(3) M9670-641 **(4)** A9650- 10
(5) L92U **(6)** AD
(7) C16 X46 X98 249 424
432 454 567 650 689
695 939 982
09991

The VIN can also be found in three other places on the car. The first is on a plate fitted at the front left corner of the dash and visible through the windscreen. The second is stamped into the bodyshell to the left of the battery (as you look at it) behind a clear plastic cover, while the third is on a label in the driver's side door catch post.

The following pages show tables of country, options, engine and transmission, and paint codes. *996*

Country Codes

Code	Country
C00	Germany
C02	Rest of USA (in 1991 became all of USA)
C03	California
C04	Puerto Rico
C05	France
C06	French colonies
C07	Italy
C08	Japan (LHD)
C09	Sweden
C10	Switzerland
C11	Austria
C12	Denmark
C13	Finland
C14	Taiwan
C15	Hong Kong
C16	Great Britain
C17	British service personnel stationed in Germany
C18	Japan (RHD)
C19	Luxemburg
C20	Holland
C21	Norway
C22	Belgium
C23	Australia
C24	New Zealand
C26	South Africa
C27	Spain
C28	Greece
C31	Saudi Arabia
C32	Arab Gulf States
C36	Canada
C45	Singapore
C69	France (pre-1986)
C72	Switzerland (pre 1986)
C98	non-specific RHD production (Cyprus, etc)
C99	Special

Option Codes

Option Code	Description
IXAA	Aerokit Cup
IXAB	Spyder rear in body colour
IXAF	Turbo aerokit
IXAG	Carrera rear spoiler
IXCA	Dashboard trim strip (3 part) sports seats
IXCC	Side air vents sports seats
IXCD	Centre air vent bracket sports seats
IXCE	Rear centre console sports seats
IXCG	Sports seat backrest in Aluminium Look finish
IXCZ	Short shifter
IXD9	Wheel painted in body colour
IXEA	Passive handset in leather
IXE8	Gear lever knob aluminium/dark burr maple/leather
IXE9	Handbrake lever aluminium/dark burr maple/leather
IXJB	Rear section of centre console in Arctic Silver
IXJ4	Leather cover for ignition lock surround
IXKB	Side air vent in light burr maple
IXKC	Side air vent in dark burr maple
IXKD	Side air vent in Carbon
IXKE	Side air vent in Arctic Silver
IXKG	Defroster trim in light burr maple; leather
IXKH	Defroster trim in dark burr maple; leather
IXKJ	Defroster trim in Carbon/leather
IXKL	Leather speaker covers
IXKM	Speaker covers in light burr maple
IXKN	Speaker covers in dark burr maple
IXKP	Carbon speaker covers
IXKR	Centre air vent bracket in light burr maple
IXKS	Centre air vent bracket in dark burr maple
IXKW	Centre nozzle bracket arctic silver
IXKX	Instrument surround in Arctic Silver
IXLA	Boxster tailpipe
IXLF	Sports exhaust system

IXMA	Rooflining in leather	IXNX	Carbon trim strip (dashboard)	IXSD	Front seat controls in leather
IXME	Rear section of centre console painted	IXNY	Trim strip in Arctic Silver	IXSE	Bucket seat, left
IXMF	Front centre console including 2 storage bins, leather	IXN3	Dashboard side air vent in leather	IXSF	Bucket seat, right
IXMF	Front centre console including 2 storage bins, leather	IXPA	3-spoke sports steering wheel in leather interior co	IXSG	Racing bucket seat, left
IXMJ	Rear section of centre console in Carbon	IXPB	3-spoke sports steering wheel, light burr maple, leather	IXSJ	6-point harness
IXMK	Roll-over bar in exterior color	IXPB	3-spoke sports steering wheel, light burr maple, leather	IXSL	6-point safety catch
IXML	Rear centre console in light burr maple	IXPC	3-spoke sports steering wheel, dark burr maple, leather	IXSM	Racing safety cage
IXML	Rear centre console in light burr maple	IXPC	3-spoke sports steering wheel, dark burr maple, leather	IXSN	Omission of rear seats
IXMP	Leather sun visor, 2 illuminated vanity mirrors	IXPD	3-spoke sports steering wheel, Carbon/leather	IXSR	Carbon back for bucket seat, right
IXMP	Leather sun visor, 2 illuminated vanity mirrors	IXPD	3-spoke sports steering wheel, Carbon/leather	IXSS	Carbon back for bucket seat, left
IXMR	Sun visor in leather, 2 illuminated vanity mirrors,	IXPG	3-spoke sports steering wheel, sports seats	IXSU	Upholstered seat
IXMY	Roll-over bar in Arctic Silver	IXPG	3-spoke sports steering wheel, sports seats	IXSW	Seat belts in Maritime Blue
IXMZ	Rear section of centre console in leather	IXPP	Loudspeaker finisher on switch panel in interior colour	IXSX	Seat belts in Guards Red
IXMZ	Rear section of centre console in leather	IXPP	Loudspeaker finisher on switch panel in interior colour	IXSY	Seat belts in Speed Yellow
IXNB	Rear centre console in dark burr maple	IXPW	Instrument surround in light burr maple	IXTC	Door panel parts in leather
IXNB	Rear centre console in dark burr maple	IXPW	Instrument surround in light burr maple	IXTE	Door panel parts in carbon/leather
IXNG	Instrument surround in leather	IXPX	Instrument surround in dark burr maple	IXTF	Door panel parts in arctic silver/leather
IXNH	Side vent, left/right defroster trim in leather	IXPX	Instrument surround in dark burr maple	IXTF	Door panel parts in arctic silver/leather
IXNH	Side vent, left/right defroster trim in leather	IXPY	Carbon instrument surround	IXTG	Inner door sills in leather
IXNN	Centre air vent bracket in leather	IXRA	17-inch Sport Classic wheel	IXTJ	Door panel parts in light burr maple
IXNR	Carbon centre air vent bracket	IXRB	18-inch Sport Classic II wheel	IXTK	Door panel parts in dark burr maple
IXNS	Leather steering column trim, 4-part	IXRC	18-inch Sport Techno wheel	IXTL	Door panel parts in Carbon
IXNS	Leather steering column trim, 4-part	IXRL	18-inch Sport Design wheel	IXTR	Door panel parts in Aluminium Look finish
IXNU	Leather trim strip (dashboard)	IXRN	17mm spacers, rear	IXTR	Door panel parts in Aluminium Look finish
IXNV	Trim strip (dashboard) in light burr maple	IXRP	5mm spacers, front/rear	IXV1	Defroster trim in leather
IXNV	Trim strip (dashboard) in light burr maple	IXSA	Painted sports seat backrest	IXX1	Floor mats, logo, leather border
IXNW	Trim strip (dashboard) in dark burr maple	IXSB	Leather sports seat backrest	IXX2	Illuminated footwell
IXNW	Trim strip (dashboard) in dark burr maple	IXSC	Porsche Crest embossed in headrest	IXY5	Tiptronic gear selector gate in leather

IXZD	Interior light surround in leather
IX45	Instrument dial in interior colour
IX46	Tiptronic selector lever in aluminium/leather
IX47	Gear lever knob in Carbon/leather
IX48	Tiptronic selector lever in Carbon/aluminium
IX51	Powerkit 250 kW
IX58	Handbrake lever in Carbon/leather
IX65	Tiptronic selector lever in light burr maple/aluminium
IX66	Tiptronic selector lever in dark burr maple/aluminium
IX69	Door entry guards in Carbon with logo
IX70	Door entry guards in stainless steel with logo
IX71	Instrument dial painted/Aluminium Look finish
IX72	Gear lever knob aluminium/light burr maple/leather
IX73	Turbo sports suspension
IX74	Sports suspension (exclusive)
IX75	Differential lock (exclusive)
IX76	Inner door sill guard, left/right
IX91	Handbrake lever aluminium/light burr maple/leather
IX97	Gear lever knob in aluminium/leather

IX98	Handbrake lever in aluminium/leather
IX99	Natural leather
I029	Standard chassis
I211	Licence plate holder version 3
I415	18-inch Turbo-Look II wheel
M004	GT3 RS (street)
M014	Sport package 996
M024	Version for Greece
M030	Sport-Type chassis
M032	Touring suspension
M034	Version for Italy
M058	Impact absorbers, front and rear
M061	Version for Great Britain
M062	Version for Sweden
M063	Version Luxemburg
M064	Version for Netherlands
M065	Version for Denmark
M066	Version for Norway
M067	Version for Finland
M068	Version for Thailand
M069	Other country version
M071	EU country version
M072	Version for Mexico
M073	Version for Russia
M094	Special model Millennium
M095	Special model '911 Anniversary Edition'

M111	Version for Austria
M113	Version for Canada
M114	Version for Taiwan
M119	Version for Spain
M124	Version for France
M126	Control and indications in French lettering
M127	Control and indications in Swedish
M130	Control and indications in English lettering
M139	Seat heating system, left seat
M150	Operation with leaded gas
M193	Version for Japan
M197	Stronger battery
M215	Version for Saudi Arabia
M219	Differential
M220	Locking differential 40%
M222	Anti-slip regulation (ASR)
M224	Automatic limited slip differential
M225	Version for Belgium
M249	Tiptronic transmission
M265	Automatic anti-dazzle interior mirror with rain sensor
M266	Automatic anti-dazzle door mirror
M270	Door mirror – flat – driver's side, elec. adjust and heat
M271	Door mirror – aspherical – driver's side, elec. adjust and heat

M273	Door mirrors, electrically adjustable and heatable
M274	Vanity mirror illuminated
M277	Version for Switzerland
M288	Headlamp washer
M320	Radio Porsche CR 11 ROW
M321	Radio Porsche CR 22
M322	Radio Porsche CR 220
M325	Version for South Africa/New Zealand
M326	Radio Porsche CR 21 ROW
M327	Radio Porsche CR 2200
M329	Radio Porsche CR 210 USA
M330	Radio Porsche CR 31 ROW
M335	Automatic seat belt, 3-point, rear
M338	Rear-wheel drive
M339	All-wheel drive
M340	Seat heating system, right seat
M342	Seat heating system, left/right seat
M369	Standard seat, left
M370	Standard seat, right
M375	Sports seat, backrest shell, left
M376	Sports seat, backrest shell, right
M392	17-inch Carrera wheel
M396	Cast wheel, 17-inch
M399	17-inch Carrera - 4 wheel
M408	18-inch Techno wheel
M411	18-inch Carrera wheel
M413	18-inch Turbo Look wheel

M414	18-inch Turbo Look wheel, high gloss finish
M417	18-inch Carrera wheel, polished
M421	Front cassette compartment
M422	Rear cassette compartment
M424	CD compartment
M425	Rear window wiper
M432	Steering wheel with Tiptronic control
M436	3-spoke airbag steering wheel
M437	Comfort seat, left, electrically adjustable
M438	Comfort seat, right, electrically adjustable
M439	Electrical hood operation
M440	Manual antenna, 4 loudspeakers (MY 2002)
M440	Antenna diversity (MY 2003)
M441	Radio preparation
M446	Concave wheel centres with full-colour Porsche Crest
M450	Ceramic brake (PCCB)
M454	Automatic speed control
M465	Rear foglamp, left
M466	Rear foglamp, right
M476	Porsche Stability Management (PSM)
M479	Version for Australia
M480	6 speed manual transmission
M484	Version for USA

M488	Inscriptions in German language
M490	Sound system (-MY01)
M490	Sound system Harmann analog (MY02)
M492	Headlamps for left-hand traffic
M498	Deletion of model designation on rear end
M499	Version for Germany
M509	Fire extinguisher
M513	Lumbar support, right seat
M532	Alarm system remote control omitted
M533	Radio convertible-top operation omitted
M534	Theft security system
M535	Anti-theft lock 315 MHz
M536	Alarm siren and tilt sensor
M537	Seating position control for comfort seat, left
M538	Seating position control for comfort seat, right
M539	Mechanical seat-height adjustment, left
M540	Mechanical seat-height adjustment, right
M549	Roof Transport System
M550	Hard top
M551	Wind deflector
M553	Version for USA, Canada

M562	Airbag, driver's side and front passenger's side
M563	Side airbag
M566	Front fog lights, white
M567	Windscreen tinted, upper part darker coloured
M571	Activated charcoal filter
M573	Air conditioner
M574	Without air conditioner
M580	Non-smoker's package
M581	Centre console, front
M586	Lumbar support, left seat
M590	Power lid locking
M601	Litronic headlights
M602	Raised stop lamp
M605	Headlight levelling system
M606	Daytime driving lights
M614	Preparation for telephone installation (Motorola 2200)
M618	Preparation for telephone installation
M620	Electronic accelerator
M635	Parking assistant
M650	Electrical sliding roof
M651	Electric window opener
M652	Without electric sunroof
M657	Power assisted steering
M659	On-board computer
M660	OBD 2

M661	Stricter emission-control concept
M662	Info/navigation system
M663	Passive handset
M664	ORVR
M665	PCM2 basic module including radio
M666	PCM2 telephone (GSM)
M668	PCM2 telephone handset
M670	PCM2 navigation
M680	Digital sound package (-MY 01)
M680	Sound system Bose (MY 02-)
M685	Rear seats, split
M686	Radio Porsche CDR 21 ROW
M688	Radio Porsche CDR 210 USA
M689	Preperation of cd autochanger
M692	CD autochanger Porsche
M695	CD radio Porsche CDR 22
M696	CD radio Porsche CDR 220
M698	CD radio Porsche CDR 32
M699	MD radio Porsche MDR32
M936	Seat covers, rear, leather
M937	Seat covers, rear, leatherette
M939	Seat covers, rear, draped leather
M946	Seat covers, front, leather/ leatherette
M981	Leather equipment without seat covers
M982	Seat covers, front, draped leather
M983	Seat covers, front, leather
M990	Seat covers, front, cloth/leatherette

M999	Passenger compartment monitoring sensor in leather colour of choice

Interior Codes

First Digit of Interior Code	Colour
3	Natural Grey
4	Natural Brown or Cashmere Beige
6	Classic Grey
7	Black
8	Black
99	Leather to Sample
A	Black
B	Space Grey
C	Graphite Grey
D	Natural Dark Grey
E	Metropole Blue
G	Metropole Blue
J	Nephrite Green
M	Boxster Red
P	Cinnamon Brown

Engine Codes

Engine Code	kW	HP	Ltr	Cyl	MY	Model	Number range
M96.01	220	300	3,40	6	1998	911 Carrera	66W 00501 >60000
M96.01	220	300	3,40	6	1999	911 Carrera	66X 00501 >60000
M96.02	220	300	3,40	6	1999	911 Carrera	468X 00501 >60000
M96.04	220	300	3,40	6	2000	911 Carrera	2/466Y 00501 >60000
M96.76	265	360	3,60	6	2000	996 GT	363Y 21501 >23000
M96.70	340	462	3,60	6	2001	911 Turbo GT	2641 00501 >60000
M96.04	220	300	3,40	6	2001	911 Carrera 2/4	661 00501 >60000
M96.70	309	420	3,60	6	2001	911 Turbo	641 00501 >60000
M96.76	265	360	3,60	6	2001	996 GT	3631 21501 >23000
M96.70	309	420	3,60	6	2002	911 Turbo	642 00501 >60000
M96.70	340	462	3,60	6	2002	911 Turbo GT2	642 00501 >60000
M96.03	235	320	3,60	6	2002	911 Carrera 2/4/4S	662 00501 >60000
M96.03	235	320	3,60	6	2003	911 Carrera 2/4/4S	663 00501 >60000
M96.70	309	420	3,60	6	2003	911 Turbo	643 00501 >60000
M96.70	340	462	3,60	6	2003	911 Turbo GT2	643 20501 >60000
M96.70	309	420	3,60	6	2004	911 Turbo	644 00501 >60000
M96.70	340	462	3,60	6	2004	911 Turbo GT2	644 20501 >60000
M96.03	235	320	3,60	6	2004	911 Carrera 2/4/4S	664 00501 >60000
M96.79	280	381	3,60	6	2004	996 GT 3	634 24501 >26000
M96.79	280	381	3,60	6	2004	996 GT 3RS	634 26501 >27000
M96.79	280	381	3,60	6	2005	996 GT 3	635 24501 >26000
M96.70	309	420	3,60	6	2005	911 Turbo	645 00501 >60000

Transmission Codes

Transmission Code	Type	Model Year(s)	Model	Number Range
G96.00	6 Speed	1998-1999	911 Carrera	G9600 1 002001 >999999
G96.00	6 Speed	1998-1999	911 Carrera M 220	G9600 2 002001 >999999
A96.00	5 Speed	1998-1999	911 Carrera Tiptronic	A9600 1 002001 >999999
G96.30	6 Speed	1999-2001	911 Carrera 4	G9630 1 002001 >999999
A96.30	5 Speed	1999-2001	911 Carrera 4 Tiptronic	A9630 1 002001 >999999
G96.90	6 Speed	2000-2001	996 GT3	G9690 2 002001 >999999
G96.00	6 Speed	2000-2001	911 Carrera 2	G9600 1 002001 >999999
A96.00	5 Speed	2000-2001	911 Carrera 2 Tiptronic	A9600 1 002001 >999999
G96.93	6 Speed	2001	996 GT3	G9693 2 002001 >999999
G96.50	6 Speed	2001-2005	911 Turbo	G9650 1 002001 >999999
A96.50	5 Speed	2001-2005	911 Turbo Tiptronic	A9650 1 002001 >999999
G96.88	6 Speed	2001-2005	911 Turbo GT2	G9688 2 002001 >999999
G96.01	6 Speed	2002-2005	911 Carrera 2	G9601 1 002001 >999999
G96.31	6 Speed	2002-2005	911 Carrera 4	G9631 1 002001 >999999
A96.10	5 Speed	2002-2005	911 Carrera 2 Tiptronic	A9610 1 002001 >999999
A96.35	5 Speed	2002-2005	911 Carrera 4 Tiptronic	A9635 1 002001 >999999
G96.96	6 Speed	2004-2005	996 GT3	G9696 2 002001 >999999

Paint Codes

	Water Based Paint	Conventional Paint	MY98	MY99	MY00	MY01	MY02	MY03	MY04
Solid Colours									
Glacier White	3AU	3AT	●	●					
Biarritz White	9A2	9A3			●	●			
Carrara White	B9A	B9A					●	●	

	Water Based Paint	Conventional Paint	MY98	MY99	MY00	MY01	MY02	MY03	MY04
Black	41	41					●	●	
Guards Red	84A	80K	●	●	●	●	●	●	
Pastel Yellow	12M	12L	●	●					
Speed Yellow	12H	12G		●	●	●	●	●	
Metallic/Pearl Colour									
Black Metallic	744	746	●	●	●	●			
Basalt Black Metallic	C9Z	C9Z					●	●	
Arctic Silver Metallic	92U	92T	●	●	●	●	●	●	
Ocean Blue Metallic	3AZ	3AY	●	●	●				
Ocean Jade Metallic	25K	25H	●	●					
Zenith Blue Metallic	3AX	3AW	●	●	●				
Lapis Blue Metallic	3A8	3A9				●	●		
Lapis Blue Metallic	M5W	M5W						●	●
Rainforest Green Metallic	2A1	2A2			●	●	●		
Arena Red Metallic	84S	84R	●	●	●				
Orient Red Metallic	843	8A4				●	●	●	
Zanzibar Red Pearl Effect	1A	1A9		●	●	●	●		
Meridian Metallic	6A6	6A7				●	●	●	
Vesuvio Metallic	40X	40W	●	●	●				
Paladio Metallic	555	554	●	●	●				
Seal Grey Metallic	6B4	6B5				●	●	●	
Midnight Blue Metallic	39C	37W							●
Lagoon Green Metallic	M6W								●
Special Colours									
Dark Blue	3C7	347		●	●	●			

	Water Based Paint	Conventional Paint	MY98	MY99	MY00	MY01	MY02	MY03	MY04
Violet ChromaFlair	3C5	3C4			●				
Wimbledon Green Metallic	2B6	23L		●	●	●			
Pine Green Metallic	2B4	22E		●	●	●	●	●	
Violet Metallic	3AE	39G		●	●	●			
Cobalt Blue Metallic	3C8	37U		●	●	●	●	●	
Polar Silver Metallic	92M	92E		●	●	●	●	●	
Slate Metallic	23F	22D		●	●	●	●	●	
Midnight Blue Metallic	39C	37W		●	●	●	●		
Zanzibar Red Pearl Effect	1A8	1A9						●	

MY 2000 Millennium Edition Interior

Note the 'bumperettes' fitted to this US spec Targa

Controls and instruments

The layout of the controls on early 911s developed over many years, and ended up as a seemingly haphazard arrangement of switches and levers, many of which are still a mystery to most owners! The 996 layout is far more ergonomic, but even so requires some understanding and explanation.

The photos show a left hand drive car, and generally speaking a right hand drive car mirrors the layout. Working from right to left:

● Passenger air vent and interior temperature sensor below it
● Above the vent is the dash loudspeaker
● Passenger airbag
● On facelift models, glovebox is below
● Centre air vent
● Centre console (see later)
● Hazard warning switch
● Instrument cluster
● Steering wheel with reach adjust below
● Dash loudspeaker (to front left)
● Ignition switch
● Driver's air vent
● Light switch – note early cars with

996 dash layout

halogen lights have a level adjuster to the right of the switch
● Door mirror adjustment (on door)

The centre console contains a variety of controls and equipment, depending on the specification, but working from the top will include some of the following:

In the "Horseshoe"
RHS
● Central locking switch
● Heated rear window
● Rear screen wiper
● Convertible top
● Cigarette lighter

LHS
● TC/PSM switch
● Rear spoiler
● Sports exhaust
● Footwell lighting
● Wiper delay/sensitivity

In the centre position
● Cupholders (facelift models)
● Air conditioning controls

● Radio
● PCM
● Storage pocket
● CD or cassette storage
● DSP controls

In the "Batwing" at the base of the console
● Heated seats (L & R)
● Targa roof
● Targa blind

On the rear centre console, behind the gear lever:
● Front windows
● Ash tray or non-smokers tray
● Rear windows (cabriolet)
● Targa rear release
● Handbrake
● Centre storage compartment

By the driver's door entry:
● Front compartment release
● Engine compartment release
● Seat/mirror position memory buttons
  Note – early 996s have longer mechanical compartment release levers.

Control panel by driver's door

The instrument cluster houses five dials, containing many analogue and digital displays. The main instruments are, from left to right:
● Battery voltage meter
● Analogue and digital speedometers
● Tachometer, digital odometer, trip and On-Board Computer display
● Engine water temperature, fuel level gauge, Tiptronic display and digital clock
● Oil pressure
There are two knobs at the top of the cluster. The left one is for adjusting the brightness of the backlighting

Instrument cluster (facelift model) with oil level showing on OBC display

and resetting the trip. The one on the right is used for setting the clock. This knob is also used to change the digital speedometer and odometer from miles to kilometres. Turn the control to the left for five seconds until the display changes. Repeat the process to switch

back. On facelift cars this is controlled through the OBC.

On the right of the instrument cluster is the telephone microphone (if fitted).

The speedometer also contains the green cruise control readiness light, and the tachometer has a blue main beam

warning light at the top, and green left/right arrow indicator warning lights. There is also a sensor for the lighting illumination.

The fuel gauge has an amber light to warn of low fuel level (10-12 litres remaining). Carrera 4 and Turbo models use a 'saddle' shaped fuel tank, due to the

The symbols (from the left) are:

	Washer fluid level warning light		Parking brake warning light		Retractable rear spoiler warning light
	Check engine warning light		Brake pad wear warning light		Luggage/engine compartment/ Targa rear lid warning light
	PSM information light		Engine oil pressure warning light		Convertible top warning light
	PSM warning light (or T/C warning light)		Battery warning light		Rollover protection system warning light
	ABS warning light		Safety belt warning light		
	Brake fluid level/brake distribution warning light		Airbag warning light		

Note – symbols may vary with model year.

Left hand stalk

4WD system. On these models, the fuel level sender will only read down to a level of 19 litres (5 US galls) and from there on the level is calculated by the instrument cluster, based on OBC data. Therefore, if the fuel level is low, adding a few litres may not bring it up to the level of the sender and the gauge will show the same level as before the fuel was added. To avoid this, always add more than 19 litres. Another point to note is that if the battery is disconnected with a low fuel level, when reconnected the fuel gauge will read around 1/4 tank, so there is a danger of running out of fuel. This also applies to GT models which use the Carrera 4 chassis.

The temperature gauge has a red warning light which has four functions:
1. Engine coolant level too low - light flashes slowly (0.5 Hz).
2. Engine compartment temperature too high - light flashes slowly (0.5 Hz) (engine compartment blower might be faulty).
3. Engine coolant temperature too high - light is lit; pointer on the right.

4. Temperature sensor at water outlet faulty - light flashes rapidly (1 Hz); pointer on the right.

Along the base of the instrument cluster is a series of warning lights. These illuminate when the ignition is switched on, but should extinguish when the engine is started. The spoiler warning light will extinguish when the car starts to move. On facelift models, should a warning light come on during normal driving, it will be accompanied by a message in the OBC.

Depending on equipment level, there are up to four control stalks on the steering column:

The upper left stalk controls the left/right indicators, and headlight beams. The central position is for dipped beams - push forward for main beams and pull back to flash main beams.

The lower left stalk controls the On-Board Computer functions in the tachometer display. Moving the lever up and down toggles the OBC modes. Pushing forward confirms a selection, and pulling towards you steps backwards.

Pre-facelift 996s have a fairly basic, but very useful, OBC system with the following functions:

● Outside air temperature
● Range on remaining fuel
● Average speed
● Average fuel consumption
● Speed warning gong

Facelift models have a far more comprehensive system, with more features, and warning messages when faults occur. In addition to the above, these functions are also available, depending on equipment fitted:

● Engine boost pressure (Turbo)
● Navigation information
● Check for stored warning messages
● Oil level check
● Telephone information
● Setting of display and units
● Switch OBC display off

The upper right hand stalk controls the windscreen wipers. From the 'off' position,

moving the lever down switches to intermittent operation, the delay of which is adjusted by the control on the 'horseshoe' panel. If rain sensor wipers are fitted, this control adjusts the sensitivity. Moving the lever up from the 'off' position switches the windscreen wipers to slow operation and moving it up one further position switches to fast operation. Pulling the lever towards you operates the windscreen washers. Pushing it away from you operates the headlamp washers (if the car is Litronic or Xenon equipped), provided the headlights are switched on. The headlamp washer nozzle covers have a nasty habit of flying off when they are operated at high speed, so I would suggest not using them at speeds above 50mph (80kph).

The lower right hand stalk operates the cruise control system. The system is activated by pressing the switch on the end of the stalk, which will illuminate the green readiness light in the speedometer. The system can be engaged at speeds between 25 and 120mph. Bring the car to the required speed and push the lever forward to set the cruise control. Pushing

Right hand stalk

RHD dash layout

16mph for over 20 seconds
● Speed falls to 5mph below the set speed for over 5 seconds

Retrofit of OBC and Cruise Control

Depending on the model and the region where the car was supplied, OBC and Cruise Control were either standard or cost options. Both functions can be retrofitted, either by specialist Porsche workshops, or by doing it yourself. There are several sources of instructions on the Internet, the most notable being on RennTech.org. In most cases it is actually cheaper to retrofit the systems than it was to specify them on the original order!

Note that early (MY1998 & 1999) Carrera 2s had a mechanical cruise control system which, although possible to fit, is far more complicated and expensive to fit. All later cars were fitted with electronic throttle (eGas) and the controls are incorporated in the DME and instrument cluster and simply need connecting and activating. 996

the lever forward briefly will cause the car to accelerate until the lever is released. Pushing and holding the lever downwards will reduce the cruise speed until it is released. Pulling it towards you briefly will interrupt cruise control. If cruise is interrupted, the speed can be resumed

by pressing the lever downwards briefly. Cruise is interrupted by:
● Briefly pulling the lever towards you
● Pressing the brake pedal
● Pressing the clutch pedal
● Selecting N on a Tiptronic
● Speed exceeds the set speed by

Owner checks

There is no doubt that improvements in quality of design, materials, machining, seals and lubricants has resulted in a significant reduction in consumption of essential fluids. I recall that in my early driving days, I would do what was almost the equivalent of an annual inspection before setting off on a 500+ mile tour. These days we have become a little complacent about making regular checks of fluid levels and sadly, the checks only get done when a small puddle appears on the garage floor!

Regular checks are a good precautionary measure and can give some advance warning of a problem. Always follow the correct procedure to avoid false readings.

Oil Level – Carrera Models

This can be done using the level display on the instrument cluster, or using the dipstick. The oil tank is integral to the engine crankcase, so the check should be done with the oil at operating temperature, but with the engine stopped and after sufficient time has elapsed for the oil to

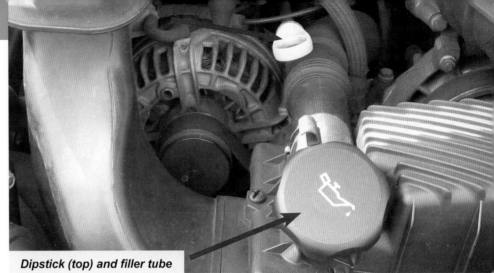

Dipstick (top) and filler tube

drain back into the crankcase. The car should be on level ground.

On pre-facelift cars, the oil level check will appear in the display immediately the ignition is switched on. On first start-up, the level will be displayed after a few seconds. If the engine has run for a short while, this time will be extended significantly. The level will also display after refuelling.

On facelift cars, the level is checked using the OBC. The level check is not performed automatically at start-up and

although it is checked during refuelling, the display will only show a reminder to check the level if it is low.

Each bar on the display is around 0.2 litres. The level can also be checked with the dipstick, to the left of the filler tube in the engine compartment.

Remove the dipstick and wipe it dry with a cloth. Push the dipstick back into the tube until it hits the stop, and withdraw it. Read off the level, which should fall between the two marks. The difference between Min(imum) and

Max(imum) is approximately 1.25 litres, the same as the upper and lower bars of the instrument display.

If necessary, add oil 0.25 litres at a time into the filler tube, allowing a few minutes for it to drain into the crankcase before re-checking.

Check the 'O' ring seal in the filler cap is undamaged and secure before replacing the cap.

Oil Level –
Turbo and GT Models

These engines have a dry sump and the oil is stored in a tank externally mounted on the engine. When the engine is running, scavenge pumps return oil from the crankcase and cylinder heads to the tank. Therefore, the oil level must be checked when the engine is running, up to operating temperature, and on level ground.

Turbo models are not supplied with a dipstick, so the check must be made on the OBC. The GT3 does have a dipstick, which is located under the cap of the filler tube. The method of checking is the same as above.

Coolant tank

Coolant Level

Always check the coolant level when the engine is cold, and the car is on level ground. The level should be within the Min and Max markings.

Never open the coolant cap when the engine is hot. Even when cold, open the cap slowly to release the pressure before removing it.

If necessary, top up with Porsche coolant (as it contains a lubricant for the coolant pump). This is a concentrate and requires dilution of 50:50 with water.

Early expansion caps are prone to blowing off at too low a pressure. This results in the loss of a small amount of water into the catch tray on top of the tank, which drains down a rubber tube to

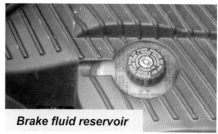

Brake fluid reservoir

the underside of the car. This quite often happens after a faster run.

The coolant tanks are also prone to cracks and pinholes, usually in the face of the tank up against the engine compartment wall. Look for the tell-tale sign of dampness under the tank.

Power Steering Fluid

The level should be checked with a cold engine – at around 20°C. To check the level, start the engine and let it idle for around 20 seconds. Switch off the engine and remove the reservoir cap. Wipe the dipstick, replace and remove again. The level should lie in the area marked "Cold".

If you need to add fluid, only use Pentosin CHF 11 S fluid.

Clutch Fluid – Turbo Models

Manual transmission Turbo models have a hydraulically assisted clutch. The power steering pump provides the pressure for the system. It has a separate reservoir located in the front compartment under the panel next to the battery, on the driver's side of the car. A single T20 Torx screw holds the panel in place.

The reservoir level should be between the Min and Max marks. Top-ups should be made with Pentosin CHF 11 S.

Screen Washer Fluid

The screen and headlamp washers share a common storage tank with around 6.5 litres capacity. This is located under the left hand font wing (fender).

A warning light will illuminate on the dash when the level drops to about 0.5 litres. This will also be accompanied by an OBC message in facelift cars.

Top up using a good quality screen wash of the appropriate concentration to give adequate anti-freeze properties.

Brake Fluid

The brake fluid reservoir is located in the front luggage compartment.

Although there is a low level warning light in the instrument cluster, this will only come on when the level has reached a dangerously low reading.

It is normal for the level to slowly go down as the brake pads wear, as more fluid will be required to fill the caliper cylinders. However, the level should be kept between the Min and Max markings at all times. If the level falls quickly between checks, this requires immediate investigation.

Top-ups should be done with an approved brake fluid. Be very careful when handling brake fluid as it is highly corrosive to paintwork and other materials.

Always check the age of the top-up fluid and screw the cap on tightly after use. Brake fluid absorbs water from the atmosphere, lowering its boiling point. This has an adverse effect on braking.

Tyre Pressures

See "Wheels and Tyres" 996

Power steering pump

Clutch reservoir - Turbo

Screen wash filler

Engine oils

Porsche regularly issue an Approved Oils List for use in its production vehicles (1984 on), with the exception of the Cayenne V6, that is based on performance and region of operation. Oil manufacturers are granted approval for a period of between 2 and 3 years, after which the manufacturer has to request an extension. The following list is an extract from the current list (which contains around 125 products), including a selection of some of the more commonly available oils.

Lubricants and fluids

Manufacturer	Trade Name	SAE Class	Sales Area
BP	BP Visco 5000	5W-40	EU, NZL, VNM, TWN
	BP Visco 5000 Turbo Diesel	5W-40	WW
	Visco 7000	0W-40	EU, Asia
	Visco 7000 Sport	5W-40	EU
	Super V Plus	5W-40	WW
CASTROL	Edge	0W-40	WW
	Edge	5W-40	WW
	Edge Professional	5W-40	WW
	Edge Sport	0W-40	WW
	Magnatec Professional C3	5W-40	WW
	SLX Professional Longtec	0W-40	EU
	Syntec	5W-40	USA, CAN
TOTAL	Quartz 9000	5W-40	WW
	Quartz 9000 Energy	5W-40	WW
	Quartz INEO MC3	5W-40	WW
ELF	Elf Solaris LSX	5W-40	WW
	Elf Excellium Full-Tech	5W-40	WW
FINA	First 400	5W-40	WW
FUCHS	Titan Supersyn	5W-40	WW
	Titan GT1	5W-40	WW
	Titan Supersyn Longlife	5W-40	WW

Manufacturer	Trade Name	SAE Class	Sales Area
EXXON/MOBIL	Esso Ultron	5W-40	WW
	Mobil 1	0W-40	WW
	Mobil 1	5W-40	WW
	Mobil 1	5W-50	WW
	Mobil Synt S	5W-40	WW
	Mobil Syst S	5W-40	WW
	Mobil 1 FF 100	0W-40	WW
	Mobil 1 Arctic	0W-40	WW
	Mobil 1 Formula C	0W-40	WW
	Mobil 1 ESP	0W-40	WW
	Mobil 1 New Life	0W-40	WW
	Mobil 1 Peak Life	5W-40	WW
	Mobil Super 3000 X1	5W-40	WW
	Mobil Super 3000 X2	5W-40	WW
MOTUL	8100 X-cess	5W-40	WW
	8100-X-clean	5W-40	WW

Engine oil capacities

Model	Capacity	Filling Quantity (with filter change)	Notes
Carrera	10.25 litres	8.25 litres approx.	After drain time of 20 minutes
Turbo	12.5 litres	8.75 litres approx.	Including turbocharger oil catch tanks
GT3	12.5 litres	8.5 litres approx.	
Also refer to your Driver's Manual			

Transmission oils

Manufacturer	Trade Name	SAE Class	Where used
Exxon/Mobil	Mobilube PTX	75W-90	Manual transmission, front axle final drive, and Tiptronic rear axle final drive – All Model Years
Shell	Transaxle	75W-90	Manual transmission, front axle final drive, and Tiptronic rear axle final drive – All Model Years

Manufacturer	Type	Where used	
Exxon/Mobil	ATF LT 71141	Tiptronic Transmission, MY1998-2001 (ZF transmission)	
Pentosin	ATF-1	Tiptronic Transmission, MY1998-2001 (ZF transmission)	
Shell	ATF 3403-M115	Tiptronic Transmission, MY2002-2005 (MB transmission)	
Fuchs	ATF 3353 or 3353 Plus	Tiptronic Transmission, MY2002-2005 (MB transmission)	

Note: The above Esso and Pentosin ATFs can be mixed, as can Shell and Fuchs ATFs, but in no other combination.

Transmission oil capacities

Transmission - Model	Where used	Capacity	Filling Quantity (approx)
G96.00 & G96.30 - C2 & C4	Manual Transmission	2.7 litres	2.7 litres
G96.50 - Turbo	Manual Transmission	3.8 litres	3.0 litres
G96.88 - GT2	Manual Transmission	3.8 litres	3.3 litres
G96.90 - GT3	Manual Transmission	3.8 litres	3.3 litres
Z96.00 - C4 & Turbo	Front Axle Final Drive	1.5 litres	1.5 litres
A96.00 & A96.30 - C2 & C4	Tiptronic Rear Axle Drive	0.9 litres	0.9 litres
A96.15/35/50 - C2, C4 & Turbo	Tiptronic Rear Axle Drive	1.2 litres	1.2 litres
A96.00 - C2 (MY98-01)	Tiptronic Transmission	9.5 litres	3.5 litres
A96.00 - C4 (MY98-01)	Tiptronic Transmission	9.0 litres	4.0 litres
A96.15/35/50 - C2, C4 & Turbo	Tiptronic Transmission	9.0 litres	4.5 litres

Other capacities

Where used	Model	Filling Capacity
Coolant	Carrera 2/4	22.5 litres *
Coolant	Turbo	28.0 litres *
Coolant	GT3	25.0 litres
Power Steering Fluid	Carrera 2/4	1.27 litres
Power Steering Fluid	GT3	1.9 litres
Power Steering & Clutch Fluid	Turbo	2.14 litres
Brake Fluid Reservoir	Carrera 2/4	0.45 litres
Brake Fluid Reservoir	Turbo	0.63 litres
Brake Fluid Reservoir	GT3	0.8 litres
* - Add approximately 1.0 litre for vehicles with Tiptronic transmission		

Other fluids and lubricants

Manufacturer	Specification/Part Number	Where used
Pentosin	CHF 11 S	Power Steering (& Clutch, Turbo only)
Porsche	000.043.203.66 (1 litre)	DOT4 Brake Fluid
Porsche	000.043.301.03 (1 litre)	Engine Coolant (Concentrate - mix 50:50 with water)
Optimoly	TA	Anti-seize compound
Porsche	000.043.204.89 (250ml)	Hydraulic Fluid for Cabriolet Top
Also refer to your Driver's Manual.		

Emergencies

Spare wheels and tools

I t is a good idea to familiarise yourself with the tool kit and spare tyre before you actually need them.

Rear wheel drive cars come with an inflated space-saver emergency wheel, mounted vertically in the front compartment. The tool kit is located in a moulded insert behind the wheel, along with the tools. Four-wheel drive cars have a non-inflated "collapsible" emergency wheel, located under the floor of the luggage compartment, along with a compressor to inflate the tyre.

GT models have a less well equipped tool kit and are supplied with a bottle of tyre foam sealant instead of an emergency wheel and jack.

All other models have a tool roll or styrofoam tray including:

● Towing eye – this screws in to the front or rear bumper, behind a plastic cover
● Box spanner/wrench for wheel bolts
● Handle for box spanner/wrench
● 10/13mm open-ended spanner/wrench
● Wheel alignment tool
● 5mm box wrench for headlight removal

Spare wheel and tool kit - 4WD models

- Double-ended screwdriver & handle
- Large plastic bag to store damaged wheel and tyre
- Pair plastic gloves

Each wheel has a locking bolt, and a wheel bolt key should be present. I put mine in the end of the box spanner/wrench in the tool roll for safe keeping and to know it will be there if I need it. Some like to keep it inside the car.

There should also be an aluminium scissor jack and handle and a red warning triangle.

I also carry a small torch. If you are touring abroad, check the specific national requirements. This might include the need for a high visibility vest, which should be kept inside the car.

There are four jacking points, located at the front and rear of each side sill (rocker panel).

If you have to use the jack, make sure the lug on the top engages fully with the slot in the jacking point.

Note the proximity of the air

Lug engages in jacking point

Emergency fuel flap release

conditioning pipes to the front right side jacking point, which can be easily damaged if the jack is misplaced.

I won't go into the detail of changing wheels, but offer the following tips:
- Ensure the handbrake is firmly engaged and no passengers remain in the car.
- Always jack on level, firm ground.
- Before taking the weight off the wheels with the jack, loosen the wheel bolts half a turn.
- Always use the wheel location tool (threaded into a wheel bolt hole). Not only does it make it easier, it also prevents

damage to the brakes – particularly if you have PCCBs.
- The car will handle significantly differently with a temporary spare wheel. Make allowances for this in your driving style.

See the section on wheels and tyres for pressures and torque settings, etc.

Fuel Flap Release

There is an emergency fuel flap release in the driver's door hinge post area (RHD). Should the fuel flap fail to unlock on the central locking system, a gentle pull of the

Positive connection in fuse panel

Negative connection to door striker

Emergency rear release cable (light unit removed)

cable should release the lock. The lock may be sprung back into position, so stand by the flap and pull the cable with one hand, while opening the flap with the other.

Flat battery?
Can't open the lids?

This is a lot more common than you might imagine. A lot of 996s are their owner's second cars, so tend to be left for longer periods between use. If the battery goes flat when the car is locked, the doors can be opened with a key, but the lids may

remain locked. This prevents access to the battery. Depending on the model of your car, there are various solutions:
1) If your car has electric lid releases, you will find a power connection in the fuse panel to connect an external battery, which will provide power to operate the alarm system. Unlock the car door with the key, and leave the key in the lock. Remove the fuse panel cover and pull out the red positive connector. Attach a jump lead from here to the positive connection on the external battery. Connect the

negative terminal of the external battery to the door striker (catch) on the B post. If the car was locked, the alarm horn will sound. Switch the alarm off by locking and unlocking with the key in the door. Unlock the lids with the regular switches and disconnect the negative followed by the positive jump leads. Do not attempt to start the car using this method!
2) If you have a facelift 996, the cigarette lighter socket is permanently live. Use a battery conditioner/charger (many have cigarette lighter plugs) to recharge the

Positive battery connection

Ground point

Emergency front release cable

battery enough to open the lids. This may take several hours.

3) There is an emergency release cable for the engine compartment lid behind the left rear light. Using a wire with a hook bent on the end, insert it into the gap along the bottom edge of the light unit, and hook out the cable. Pull the loop of the cable while lifting the rear lid. Inside the engine compartment is a positive battery connection under a hinged plastic cover. Using jump leads, connect the positive connection of the external battery

to this post and the negative to a suitable grounding point in the engine bay, such as the stud at the rear of the air filter housing. Lock and unlock the car with a key in the door lock. Unlock the front lid with the switch, or if the car has mechanical releases, the levers should now be unlocked. Disconnect the jump leads.

4) There is also an emergency release cable for the front lid, but it is much more difficult to access. On cars with mechanical releases, this is on the left hand side. Cars with electrical releases

have the cable on the right hand side. Turn the steering wheel to left or right, as appropriate to get better access to the front wheel arch liner. Remove the plastic rivets and/or self-tapping screws on the front section of the liner, so that you can pull it back far enough to get your hand inside. The cable is located at the side or base of the headlamp support tray. The accompanying photo is taken from the inside of the front wing, looking forward, and you can see the loop of the cable to the left of the tray.

Towing

A towing eye is provided in the tool kit. Remove the plastic cover in the bumper and screw in the towing eye tightly. Switch on the ignition so that the brake lights and indicators will operate. Ensure transmission is in Neutral. Always keep the tow rope taut, to avoid snatching and tow at a safe speed. For Tiptronic vehicles, do not exceed 30mph (50kph) and do not tow for more than 30 miles. There is no power assistance to the steering when towing and it will feel very heavy.

If tow-starting the car, only do this when cold to prevent damage to the catalytic converters.

If the battery is completely discharged, do not tow-start, but use jump lead starting.

Front towing eye position

Jump starting

Connect the positive (red) lead to the power terminal in the engine compartment (shown in the photo on page 51) and to the positive terminal of the external battery. Connect the negative (black) cable to the air filter housing stud and to the negative terminal of the external battery. Run the engine of the donor vehicle at a fast idle and start the engine. If the engine does not start within 15 seconds of cranking, leave for one minute before retrying. Once started, disconnect the cables in reverse order. 996

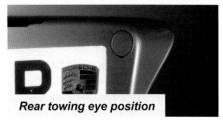

Rear towing eye position

Paintwork and wheel care

We all have our own washing and cleaning regimes, and favourite cleaning products. My 996 is my daily driver, so my regime may be different to someone who prepares their car for concours events, or maybe only uses it on dry days. However, there is some common ground and although I am not going to dwell on the finer points, I hope some of the following is useful.

Every Spring I start from scratch with the cleaning process and rely on 'top-ups' throughout the rest of the year.

I start by giving the car a jet wash with a high pressure cleaner, to remove all the accumulated dirt and debris under the wheel arches, followed by a hand wash using a good quality car shampoo, applied with a lamb's wool mitt, and a thorough rinse with a hose.

Wheels are sprayed with a solution of citrus cleaner/degreaser, which is worked in to the folds and cavities with a stiff wheel brush. Some owners go one step further and remove the wheels to

An array of products to get you started!

clean inside the rims and the back of the spokes. There are also 'rim wax' products to help keep them clean.

I dry the paintwork using large microfibre detailer's drying cloths.

Over the course of a year, the paintwork attracts a lot of minor

contaminants. I remove these with a clay bar, lubricated with a weak solution of water and car shampoo. If you haven't tried a clay bar before, you will be amazed at what it removes that you hadn't seen and how easy it is to use. The result is a perfectly prepared surface on which to apply polish or wax.

I have to admit that I like an easy life and although amazing results can be achieved using Carnauba wax, which is a popular choice, I prefer an all-in-one polish and protectant. This I apply with a towelling polish applicator pad and buff with a microfibre cloth.

Finally, I apply a spray sealant which removes any traces of polish dust and gives a high gloss shine.

During the rest of the year I just wash and dry the car, and apply a coat of polish every couple of months.

Also bear in mind that my 996 is silver, which is probably the easiest colour to keep clean. Dark colours show imperfections much more, especially 'swirl' marks in the clear coat. These can be removed using a rubbing compound and plenty of hard work, or by machine polishing. I would suggest that if you are not practised in this art, you should leave it to a professional.

If you don't plan to use the car for a day or two, it is very important that you take it for a short run after washing (and

after a jet wash in particular). Several brake applications will dry off the discs/ rotors. Damp brake discs rust very quickly, particularly on the inside faces. I can't stress this point enough, as I have seen dozens of discs that look perfectly good from the outside, but the inner faces are in a terrible condition.

Once a year, I clean the leather using a proprietary cleaner and finish with a leather conditioner. I like to drive with the window partially open. As a result I have to clean the inside of the windows with a glass polish on a regular basis and wipe the interior surfaces with a damp microfibre cloth. I won't insult you by telling you how to use a vacuum cleaner for the carpets!

However, while you have the vacuum cleaner out, take a few minutes to vacuum the debris from the inside of the front body openings, using a crevis tool. Leaves and other debris build up in this area, which inevitably turns in to a wet mulch. This builds up around the bottom of the radiators, causing them to corrode away, and eventually leak. See the following

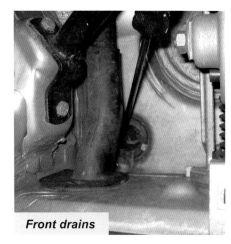
Front drains

pages for removing the front bumper (PU) to give the radiators a proper clean.

Water Drains

There are several areas where water collects and these are provided with drains. If the drains block, water can spill over into the car's interior and cause wet carpets or worse. Rather than leave it until this happens, it is worth taking the time to clear the drains.

All 996s have drains in the front

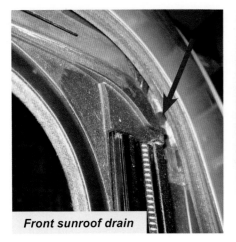

Front sunroof drain

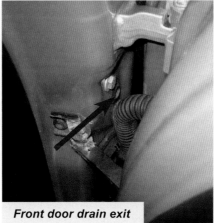

Front door drain exit

compartment, either side of the battery. These are the ones that block most commonly, with the result that water spills in to the front footwells. There are two such drains on each side and they run straight to the underside of the car, so can be carefully cleared with a screwdriver.

There is also a small drain tube under the fuel filler flap, but it is rare for it to get blocked.

There are drains around the sunroof aperture on both sides, front and back.

The front tubes run down the A pillar (windshield pillar), and out through a grommet in the front door shut, just below the top hinge. The drain tubes can be cleared by gently blowing compressed air into the top hole, or by inserting a nylon line – the sort used by a garden strimmer. If you use the air line, make sure you wear safety glasses.

The rear sunroof drain is very much more difficult to access. These tubes run from the rear of the sunroof aperture,

down the C pillar (rear screen pillar), into the engine compartment and out towards the ground. Fortunately, it is also more difficult for debris to reach the top end, so unless you are having problems they are probably best left alone.

Water in the cabriolet top storage area is collected in a tray at each side. With the top in the service position (half raised) the trays can be cleaned and the tubes cleared. The tubes run from the bottom of the tray into the rear wheel arches, but the exit grommets are obscured by the wheel arch liners. If you gently blow compressed air into the top of the tube, you will be able to hear the air escaping through the grommet if the tube is clear.

A blocked rear cabriolet drain is a common cause of alarm control unit failures. Water can drain into the left hand floor, where the module is located under the seat.

Targa drains are similar to the Coupé, with a drain in the centre of the roof panel and additional drain at the bottom of the rear 'tailgate' window.

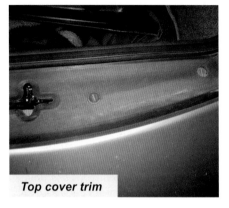

Top cover trim

Plastic rivets in wheel arch liner

Expanding rivet

Front bumper (PU) removal & radiator cleaning

Vacuuming out the debris in the front openings should be considered part of a regular cleaning regime, but it will not remove any particles trapped between the air conditioning condensers and water radiators. This can be done by removing the front PU. The PU removal procedure takes (with practice) less than half an hour, so it is worth doing this project annually to prolong the life of the radiators.

Using a flat blade screwdriver, start by removing the four ¼ turn fasteners from the top cover trim and lift off the trim. Undo the two top fixing screws with a cross-headed screwdriver. Lever out the plastic expanding rivets in the front of the wheel arch liners using a forked tool (or flat blade screwdrivers).

Unclip the side markers and unplug the bulb holder (or remove it completely by turning ¼ turn).

Remove the screw at the front of the side marker opening using a cross-headed screwdriver.

Peel back the wheel arch liner and remove the cross-headed screw that goes vertically into the back of the side marker opening.

Moving to the underside of the car, there are different fixings, dependent on the model. These photos show an early 996 with factory fitted aerokit. In this case there are seven self-tapping screws, but on other models there can be around 9 fixings that are a mixture of self tapping screws and expanding rivets.

Unclip the outside air temperature sensor from the mounting bracket in the front right hand opening.

The front PU will now slide off the front

Side marker light

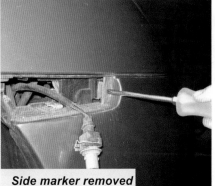

Side marker removed

Vertical screw

of the car. Removal can be a single-handed job, but for replacement it is better to have some help, so that one person can line up each side.

Now it is a case of removing the rubber shrouds for the radiators, which are fixed on with 5 cross-headed screws. Two are on the outside edge of the ducts. One is tucked out of view under the headlight unit. Finally, two are located on the inner edge near the bottom. The duct can now be removed.

The extent of the debris build-up should now be apparent, but it is a

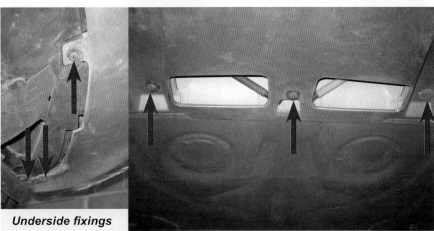

Underside fixings

Outside duct screws

Top duct screw

Lower duct screws

Condenser fixing screws

good idea to loosen the air conditioning condensers, to remove the debris behind them.

Remove the two Torx screws shown. Without disconnecting the condenser pipes you can slide the condenser out of the mounting tabs at the other end. There is some 'give' in the rubber air conditioning pipes where the aluminium ones are attached, which allows around 10mm (0.5-inch) of movement.

Gently ease the condenser away from the radiator by around 25mm (1-inch) at the outside edge. Carefully clean in between with a brush, taking

Gently separate condenser

care not to damage the fins of the matrices. If you have an air line, finish off by carefully blowing an air gun onto

the surface. Again, use safety glasses to protect your eyes.

Refitting is the reverse of the removal. 996

Maintenance

Although many of us like to 'do-it-yourself', the majority will take the car to a Porsche dealer or independent specialist for scheduled services, in order to maintain a full service history. Whilst we might do interim work, such as extra oil, or disc/rotor and pad changes, we want that all-important stamp in the Guarantee & Maintenance Booklet. The schedules can be a bit bewildering for the different models, especially as they have been revised over the years and may not exactly match what is shown in the booklet. The following table shows a summary of the latest schedules, but there are several notes and extras for each:

Annual Maintenance

Porsche advise that on vehicles with annual mileages of less than 15000 km (9000 mls), annual maintenance must be carried out once a year. In practice, the 'annual' service appears to have been replaced with just either the 'Minor' or 'Major' services outlined in the next paragraphs (and depending on the time or distance covered). It is suggested that on a low mileage (sub 9000 miles) car, maintenance with an oil filter change must be performed every 2 years (as separate from just an annual oil change). Again, in practice, when owners have the annual 'Minor' service, this usually includes the filter because of the low relative cost of replacement.

The engine oil and oil filter must be changed every 10,000 km (6,000 mls) on vehicles which are operated in countries with leaded fuel (country coding M150 in the control unit).

From the start of the 2004 model year, the annual service requirement was deleted (but see the following paragraphs).

The service schedule is all-important

Minor Maintenance

The Minor service has become the regular service where (most importantly), the oil and filter are changed. The following table details the items that are checked during a Minor service. The Minor service need is based either on time or distance covered. A minor service is due when the car is one year old or has covered 12000 miles (20000km) whichever comes the sooner. The Minor service is repeated alternately with the Major service (see next paragraph) at either years 3, 5, 7, etc or at 36000 (60000km), 60000 miles (100000km) etc. In the USA the Minor service intervals are annual or at distances of 15000 miles, 45000mls, etc..

From the start of the 2004MY (in August 2003), the intervals for the Minor/Major services remained at 12000 miles (20000km). If the mileage for scheduled maintenance is not reached, minor maintenance with oil change must be carried out after 2, 6, 10.... years. It should be noted that it was the 997/987 models that introduced the 20000 miles/30000km intervals.

The maintenance item 'Replacing spark plugs' depends on the model year.

USA only – it is extremely important to check the air cleaner (and replace it if necessary) each time minor maintenance is carried out.

The test item 'Checking inner release of luggage compartment (Trunk Entrapment)' has been added to the country specification C02 (for USA) and C36 (for Canada) as of model year 2003.

Major Maintenance

As above, plus: The maintenance item 'Throttle actuation: Check smooth operation, check full throttle position with the Tester' has been omitted as of model year 2002.

For MY2004 – if the mileage for a regular service is not reached, major maintenance must be carried out after 4, 8, 12.... years. 996

Maintenance schedules summary

Model	Type	Distance	Diagnostic System Readout	Check polyrib belt condition	Replace polyrib belt	Change engine oil	Change engine oil and filter	Replace spark plugs	MT - change transmission oil	AT - change ATF, filter and final drive oil	4WD - change oil in front drive	Change brake fluid	Cab - check rollover protection
All models up to MY2003 (not required for MY2004 on)	Annual	Less than 9000 miles per year	●										
All models	Minor	RoW - 12000, 36000, 60000 etc USA - 15000, 45000, 75000 etc or MY2004 on, every 2, 4, 6 years	●				●						
All models	Major	RoW - 24000, 48000, 72000 etc USA - 30000, 60000, 90000 etc or MY2004 on, every 4, 8, 12 years	●	●				●					
Carrera up to MY1999, all GT3 & Turbo	Additional	RoW - 24000, USA - 30000											
Carrera MY2000	Additional	RoW - 36000, USA - 45000											
Carrera MY2001 on	Additional	RoW - 48000, USA - 60000 or at least every 4 years											
Carrera up to MY2001, all GT3 & Turbo	Additional	RoW - 48000, USA - 60000											
All models	Additional	RoW - 48000, USA - 60000							●				
All models	Additional	RoW - 96000, USA - 90000								●			
All models	Additional	2 years										●	●
All models	Additional	4, 8, 10 then every 2 years											

All distances shown here are in miles

Airbag system inspection	Visual inspection of rubber mounts and bushes	Underbody inspection for leaks, panels, and damage	Inspect front inlets	Check coolant hoses, radiators and front inlets, coolant level and antifreeze	Replace air cleaner element	Check air filter - USA ONLY	Replace fuel filter	Check PAS fluid level	Replace particle filter	Visual inspection of fuel system for damage	Check engine oil level	Check parking brake free play	Check brake disks and pads	Visual inspection of brake hoses, lines, check brake fluid level	Check smooth throttle operation and full throttle position (only up to MY2002)	Check clutch for play and pedal end position	Visual inspection of steering gear bellows	Check steering tie rod ends for play and dust bellows	Check axle joints for play and dust bellows	Visually inspect drive shaft boots for leaks	Visual inspection of exhaust for leaks and damage	Check axle joints for play, dust bellows, and screw connections	Check tyres and spare wheel condition and pressures	Check function and adjustment of lighting and horn operation	Check operation of electrical equipment and warning lights	Oils, fluids, visual inspection for leaks	Check function of door locks, lid locks, safety hooks & seat belts	Check inner release of luggage compartment (USA/Canada only - from MY2003 on only)	Check windscreen wiper/washer system, fluid levels, nozzle settings, antifreeze	Report - long life guarantee	Test drive: check remote control, front seats, foot & parking brakes, engine, clutch, steering, transmission, ParkAssist, cruise control, TC/PSM switch, heating, aircon, system & instruments
		●	●					●			●			●			●	●	●	●			●	●	●	●					●
		●			●			●	●		●									●			●	●	●	●	●	●	●		●
		●		●	●			●	●				●			●	●	●	●	●	●	●	●	●	●	●	●		●		●
							●																								
																														●	
●	●																														

Engine - Mechanical

The 3.4-litre M96/0x series engine in the 996 Carrera was designed as part of a family with the 2.5-litre Boxster engine and was a completely new design. It shared no components with any previous Porsche 911. For the first time it was water cooled, ending a run of air cooled flat-six engines that had lasted over three decades.

Among many new innovations, new features included 4-valve per cylinder technology, Variocam variable inlet valve timing and Lokasil liners cast directly into the crankcase. These all helped to contribute to lower hydrocarbon emissions and fuel consumption than previous models, but with an increase in output. The double overhead camshafts on each bank were driven by duplex chains, themselves driven by an intermediate shaft driven off the crankshaft. Variocam variable valve timing is achieved by controlling the pressure feed to the adjuster mechanism on the camshaft drive with a hydraulic solenoid valve.

The all-alloy engine was cooled using two radiators that were mounted

3.4L 996 engine

at the front of the car, while cars with Tiptronic transmission had an additional central radiator.

Although described as a dry sump engine, the oil 'tank' was contained within the engine sump. An oil pump, driven from one end of the intermediate shaft, supplied oil to the bearings and cylinder head through galleries cast directly into the crankcase. The oil supply passed through a full flow filter and a water/oil heat exchanger. A camshaft-driven scavenge pump in each cylinder head returned oil to the crankcase. An oil pressure sensor was fitted to the right hand cylinder head and an oil level sensor was provided within the crankcase.

Maximum power was 300hp (220kW) at 6800rpm with a maximum torque of 350Nm (258lb.ft) at 4600rpm.

Mechanically, the 3.4 engine had few modifications during its production run, apart from a redesign of the intermediate shaft and drive.

For the MY2002 facelift the capacity was increased to 3.6-litres and Variocam

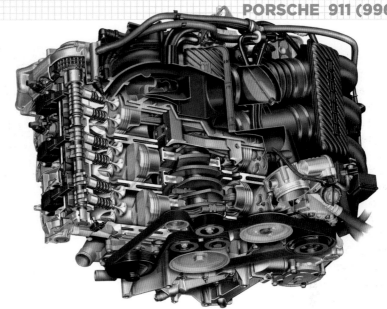

3.6L 996 engine

Plus was introduced. Variocam Plus was a significant development of the previous system. It added variable valve lift to the inlet camshafts to complement the variable valve timing.

The effect of these changes was a further improvement in power, fuel economy, emissions and smoother idling. Output increased to 320hp (235kW) at

6800rpm, with an increase in torque to 370Nm (273lb.ft) at 4250rpm.

Variable valve lift is achieved by having two camshaft profiles for each valve lobe and two-piece hydraulic tappets. A hydraulic valve controls the tappets, so that either the central section of the tappet acts on the central section of the camshaft lobe (lower lift), or the outer section of the tappet acts on the outer profiles of the camshaft lobe (higher lift).

Both the 3.4 and 3.6 Carrera engines could be optionally specified with an expensive Power Kit performance upgrade. Known as option X51, the modifications were extensive and included different camshafts, manifolds, cylinder heads, sump, an additional radiator and, in the case of the 3.4, pistons. Of course, a new fuel map was required and the total package gave an increase of around 20hp (15kW).

The X51 option could be specified on order, or retrofitted by the dealers.

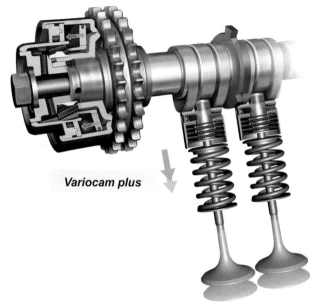

Variocam plus

The M96/70 series Turbo engine is quite different to the Carrera, with the design based on the 1998 Le Mans winning GT1 engine. With 4-valves per cylinder and twin turbochargers, one on each bank of cylinders, maximum power

was an impressive 420hp (308kW) at 6000rpm. Variocam Plus was introduced on the Turbo engine and this contributed to the engine's amazing flexibility. Maximum torque was a huge 560Nm (413lb.ft) over the range 2700-4600rpm, while economy and emissions were also improved.

The engine was a true dry sump unit, with an externally mounted oil tank. Forged aluminium pistons run in Nikasil-coated aluminium liners and were cooled with oil jets. Scavenge pumps in each cylinder head and a central scavenge pump in the crankcase returned oil to the tank. Oil was de-aerated by an oil separator within the oil tank and cooled using a

996 Turbo engine

996 GT3 engine

heat exchanger linked to the coolant system. No dipstick was provided and oil level measurement was indicated by the On-Board Computer system.

Twin K16 turbochargers with double intercoolers provided up to 0.8 bar (12psi) of intake boost pressure. Integrated wastegates in the turbine housing, controlled by vacuum actuators, were used to regulate boost pressure. The exhaust was split into two separate systems, one for each bank, with separate catalytic converters.

A total of three radiators mounted at the front of the car looked after the cooling.

A Power Kit, coded option X50, used the larger K24 turbochargers and was offered as a factory-fitted option. This elevated maximum power to 450hp (330kW) at 5700rpm, with an increase of maximum torque to 620Nm (457lb.ft) at 3500-4500rpm.

Introduced for MY2001, the 996 GT2 engine was essentially the same construction as the Turbo, but with larger K24 turbochargers and a revised fuel map. The result was an increase in power

Exhaust bypass modification

to 462hp at 5700rpm, with a torque of 620Nm (457lb.ft) at 3500-4500rpm. For MY2003, the power was increased to 483hp (355kW).

The M96/76 series engine developed for the 2000MY 996 GT3 engine was another development of the GT1 engine,

but without turbochargers.

There are many common features to the Turbo and GT3 engines, such as Variocam, Nikasil liners, dry sump, etc, but there are significant internal changes to make it a much higher revving engine. These include titanium connecting rods, lightweight pistons and lightweight valves, resulting in an engine that can be revved to 8200rpm.

When it was introduced at the end of 1999, maximum power was 360hp (265kW) at 7200rpm, with peak torque of 370Nm (272lb.ft) at 5000rpm. Maximum power was increased on the MY2004 (facelifted) models to 381hp (280kW) at 7400rpm with a maximum torque of 385Nm (284lb.ft) at 5000rpm.

The MY2004 GT3RS used exactly the same engine (M96/79) as the facelift GT3.

It has to be said that the standard Carrera exhaust is somewhat muted, and not very exciting. Many people retrofit the Porsche PSE (switchable exhaust), but in recent years the kit has become very expensive. A far cheaper solution has been carried out by many owners by modifying the standard silencers to replicate a non-switchable version of the original PSE. This involves welding a 1-inch x 16swg stainless steel tube between the inlet and outlet pipes of the silencer.

Problems and faults

Generally speaking, the M96/0x series Carrera engine is highly reliable and robust. That isn't to say that it does not have its faults, but the major ones are relatively rarely seen. Unfortunately, these faults can be exaggerated by reports on internet forums and message boards, and blown out of proportion. It is the nature of forums that few, if any, owners join one to post that their car has no problems. More likely it is an unhappy owner wishing to sound off their anger or frustration.

Nevertheless, there are some issues that I must mention.

Rear Main oil Seal (RMS)

This is the crankshaft oil seal at the flywheel end of the engine. Leaks from this seal are relatively common. Normally, it shows itself by a drip or two on the garage floor perhaps once or twice a month. Once started, the 'weep' does not tend to get significantly worse and to many owners is nothing more than an annoyance that can last for years. For some reason, Tiptronics seem to be less susceptible to the problem than manual transmission cars.

There are theories into the cause of the leak, but I believe most of these are just speculation.

Porsche have redesigned the seal and fitting tool on several occasions. The seal is now on its fifth generation, and with each design revision improvements have been noted.

Just to confuse matters, what have been reported as RMS leaks have turned out to be other causes, as they are of a similar magnitude and location. These can be the intermediate shaft support post seal or bolts, or the bolts joining the crankcase at that point.

When replacing the RMS, it is a false economy not to replace the intermediate shaft seal and bolts and the crankcase bolts. The cost of the parts is relatively small, but the cost of labour is significant.

Manual transmission cars require the removal of the transmission, clutch and flywheel, so most experts advise to wait until the clutch needs replacing, when it adds a minimal amount to the cost.

Although early Tiptronic transmissions can be removed separately, general opinion is that it is easier to remove engine and transmission in one unit, as is required for the facelift models. Although Tiptronics tend to suffer less from the problem, it is far more expensive to rectify and there is no other excuse for waiting, as with a clutch that progressively wears out.

Leaking spark plug tubes

3.4-litre engines have a plastic tube, with 'O'-ring seals at each end, to seal the cylinder head at the spark plug openings. Over time, the 'O'-rings can harden and leak, or the tubes can become brittle and crack. They are relatively cheap and easy to replace. These were eliminated on the 3.6 engine, where the passage was incorporated in the cylinder head design.

A well developed oil leak from the area under the Rear Main Seal (RMS)

Intermediate shaft failure

By far the most serious failure is that of the intermediate shaft. Failure can cause severe engine damage, especially if it happens at high engine speed. It is generally agreed that the failure is a result of the support bearing at the flywheel end of the engine breaking up, causing the shaft to break free at that end. The shaft itself can buckle, striking internal components and the loss of drive to the valve gear can cause severe damage to the pistons and cylinder heads, similar in severity to a camshaft belt failure on a conventional engine.

The shaft and bearing have been the subject of design revisions over the years, which has reduced the number of incidences, but not eliminated them entirely. The bearing is a sealed unit and there is speculation that this is the reason for the failure. It is normally accepted that an open bearing would suit the application better, as it would be lubricated by the oil circulation in the crankcase.

One theory suggests that the majority of failures are at relatively low mileages - that

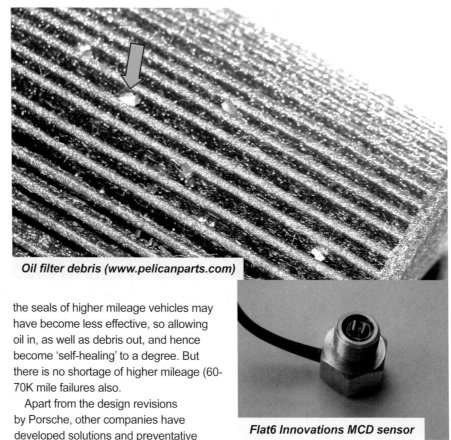

Oil filter debris (www.pelicanparts.com)

Flat6 Innovations MCD sensor

the seals of higher mileage vehicles may have become less effective, so allowing oil in, as well as debris out, and hence become 'self-healing' to a degree. But there is no shortage of higher mileage (60-70K mile failures also.

Apart from the design revisions by Porsche, other companies have developed solutions and preventative measures for the problem. Most involve a strengthened mounting post and upgraded bearing. One such solution is by LN Engineering in the USA, who supply a retrofit kit containing a hybrid ceramic bearing. Although expensive, it appears to be extremely effective.

Other than replacing the bearing, suggestions for what can be done to help prevent a failure include changing the oil on a more regular basis and thoroughly examining the used oil filter. Any metallic or plastic traces could be a sign that the bearing is failing.

Should the worst happen to you, and you do not have a warranty, then there is still hope. Over the last few years many specialists have developed techniques to rebuild and strengthen failed engines, at significantly less cost than an exchange Porsche engine.

The latest news is that an American company, Flat6 Innovations, has developed an on-board failure detection system, known as the IMS Guardian. The system has a Magnetic Chip Detector which senses ferrous metal flakes in the oil, often the first sign of an imminent intermediate shaft bearing failure, and a visual and audible warning in the cabin prior to it failing completely and doing severe damage.

Cylinder liner failure

These are extremely rare, but when it happens there appear to be two types of failure. The first is 'liner slippage' where the cylinder liner moves in the crankcase. This problem is believed to be restricted to a batch of early 3.4 cars. Slightly more often reported is the 'D-chunk' failure, where a small D-shaped section breaks off the top of the liner, on one of the middle cylinders. Again, specialist repairers have developed solutions to repair such problems.

Cylinder Liner Scoring

I cannot stress the importance of warming the engine up properly, before making the most of its performance. There have been reports of the cylinder bores becoming scored, mostly on 3.6 litre engines, resulting in high oil consumption and piston ring leakage.

Again, theories abound, but it is generally thought that it is caused by local overheating, particularly of cylinders 5 and 6 (the last on the cooling path) during warm-up, prior to the thermostat opening.

As described in the owner's manual, it is best to start the engine and drive off straight away, to warm up the catalytic converters more quickly. Keep the engine speed low (below 3000rpm) and avoid labouring the engine until the coolant reaches operating temperature. Remember that the oil takes much longer to warm up than the water. A good rule of thumb is that it takes twice as long, so keep the engine speed and load down until the engine is thoroughly warmed.

Gentle warming and avoiding excessive load will help prevent cylinder liner wear. It has also been suggested that fitting a lower temperature thermostat (71°C instead of the standard 83°C item) can help, as it opens earlier, thus getting the water circulating earlier. Such thermostats are made by Motorad in Germany, part number 460 160.

Help! Smoke!

It is always alarming to see smoke coming from the exhaust and the natural reaction is to fear the worst. However, there is often a simple and not too expensive answer.

White smoke

Vast plumes of white smoke from the exhaust is often the sign that the air/oil separator on the engine has failed. This device separates oil mist from the crankcase and returns the oil to the sump. The separator is prone to splitting inside, the mist is routed directly into the throttle body and so burned in the combustion process – resulting in the white smoke. This can happen at idle or at speed and the volume of smoke is quite alarming.

Unburned oil in the exhaust can damage the oxygen sensors, so it is advisable to have it repaired sooner rather than later.

A simple test to check for failure is to remove the inlet hose to the throttle body, open the butterfly, and look inside with a torch. If the surfaces inside are covered in oil film, it is a sure indication that the oil separator has failed.

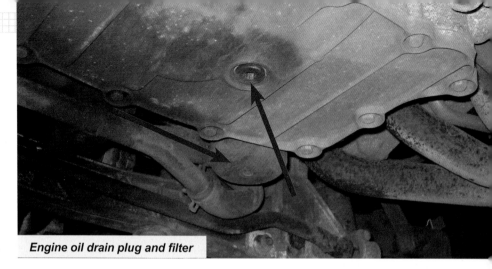

Engine oil drain plug and filter

The separator is mounded on the top of the engine, at the far end of the engine compartment, and quite difficult to access – particularly on Tiptronic cars. It is possible for the skilled enthusiast to do a DIY replacement, but it is very time consuming.

Blue smoke

It is very common to occasionally get a puff of blue smoke at start-up. It also seems to be more common on Turbo engines. This should clear in a matter of a few seconds. It is generally believed to be caused by the oil on the horizontal cylinder bores seeping past the piston rings when left overnight. This oil then burns when the car is started, giving the blue smoke.

A sure way to induce this is to get the car out of the garage, wash it, and then put it away. Next day it will probably produce such smoke.

If blue smoke persists for longer than a few seconds, I would recommend further investigation. The M96/0x Carrera engine consumes very little oil, so if consumption increases in line with smoking, it may also indicate a problem.

Filter removal tool

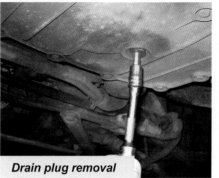

Drain plug removal

Oil filter housing removal

Oil change instructions

(Carrera models only)

You will need a drain pan of at least 10-litres (2.65 US galls) capacity, an 8mm hexagon bit tool and a filter removal tool. The Porsche 9204 removal tool, part number 000.721.920.40, is a little expensive, but a good quality 74mm 14-flute filter tool can be obtained from most tool shops at a reasonable cost.

1. Remove the oil filler cap.

2. Unscrew the oil drain plug (8mm hexagon bit). Drain the oil into an oil collection pan. Allow to drip for 20 minutes (important).

3. Clean oil drain plug and re-fit using a new aluminium sealing ring. Torque to 50Nm.

4. Undo the oil filter housing with the special tool and remove it, bearing in mind it is filled with oil. Pour the oil into the collection pan.

5. Remove the filter element. Let it drain and check the surface for debris. If any metallic or plastic debris is found, this requires urgent investigation.

6. Carefully lever off the old 'O' ring seal from the filter bowl. Do not use a pointed tool as it can damage the sealing groove of the plastic housing.

7. Clean oil filter housing on the inside and outside. Fit a new 'O'-ring and apply a film of general purpose grease to the 'O' ring.

8. Insert a new filter element and refit the oil filter housing, tightening to a torque of 25Nm.

9. Check the filling capacity in the 'Lubricants & Fluids' section.

10. Fill the engine oil slowly to avoid the oil overflowing in the filler tube. Don't forget to screw the cap on again tightly. Check the oil level with the dipstick (or on the OBC as necessary, noting the oil level measurement requirements).

Dispose of old oil responsibly and in the correct manner. 996

Engine - Electronics

DME Types

Three versions of the Bosch Motronic DME (Digitale Motor Elektronik) engine management systems were utilised on 996 models.

DME 5.2.2

This system was used on the early 3.4 litre Carrera 2 models that employed mechanical (cable) throttle actuation.

DME 7.2

DME 7.2 introduced electronic throttle control when the Carrera 4 was released and became standard on the Carrera 2 for MY2000.

DME 7.8

This was introduced on the Turbo and GT2 in MY2001 and became the standard for all models from the MY2002 facelift.

DME 5.2.2 was not truly OBDII compliant on RoW models, but US and Canada models were adapted for compliance by the addition of extra equipment:

● oxygen sensors after the catalytic converters

● secondary air system
● camshaft Hall effect (electro-magnetic) sensors for cylinders 4-6
● extended tank ventilation diagnosis with system leak test
● modified carbon canister
● complete OBDII diagnosis with activation of CEL (Check Engine Light)
● modified error memory management when CEL activated

Full OBDII compliance was achieved from version 7.2 on all models.

To go into any depth on the engine management system is beyond the scope of this book, but it may be useful to know the extent and functions of the key sensors and controls.

Sensors and Inputs:

Mass air flow sensor – a hot film sensor which measures the flow of air into the engine. Despite being described as "immune to dirt" and having a life of 100,000 miles, this is somewhat optimistic. The intake air temperature is also measured by the MAF sensor.

Engine temperature sensor – measures the temperature of the cooling water. There are two sets of contacts, one for the temperature gauge and one to inform the DME.

Throttle potentiometer – reads the position of the throttle butterfly, in particular to control the idle speed.

Throttle pedal position sensor (DME 7.x only) – mounted above the throttle pedal, linked by a cable.

Knock sensors – detect knocking combustion (pre-detonation or 'pinking'). The sensors are piezo-electric and if knocking is detected the ignition timing is adjusted accordingly.

Hall effect sensors – these read a rotor on the camshafts to determine the top dead centre position of number 1 cylinder. The signals are also used in Variocam diagnosis.

Pulse generator – reads the crankshaft rotation. This is an inductive sensor that reads the teeth of a pressed steel ring gear welded to the flywheel. The ring gear has 60 teeth, with two teeth missing to provide a reference point.

Oil temperature sensor – this is incorporated into the oil level sensor. The DME also uses the oil temperature as part of the Variocam control.

Pre-catalytic converter oxygen sensors – these monitor the oxygen values in the exhaust, feeding information to the DME that regulates the fuelling to each cylinder accordingly. They are heated by electric heaters as well as the flow of hot exhaust gases.

Post-catalytic converter oxygen sensors – these monitor the efficiency of the catalytic converters and have no control function.

Engine compartment temperature sensor – this reports the engine compartment temperature to the DME as part of the control for the engine compartment cooling fan.

Air conditioning – when switched on, signals are fed to the DME to increase idle speed and to control the cooling fans.

Vehicle speed – taken from the ABS sensors.

Brake and clutch switches – these signals are also fed to the DME.

Fuel tank pressure sensor – used during the tank venting process.

Tiptronic – there is a constant data exchange between the Tiptronic module and DME, informing it of shift operations and allowing the DME to reduce engine torque for a smoother change.

There is also interaction with the TC or PSM system.

Actuators and Outputs:

Ignition coils – each cylinder has an ignition coil mounted directly over the spark plug. Firing is controlled by the DME.

Fuel injectors – these control the amount of fuel introduced into the cylinder by adjusting the opening time.

Throttle body (DME 7.x) – the throttle butterfly is motorised and controlled by the DME.

Variocam and Variocam Plus hydraulic valves – the DME uses these to control valve lift and timing.

Idle speed control valve (DME 5.2.2 only)

Tank venting valve – this controls the extraction of fuel vapour from the carbon canister and feeds it into the intake for combustion.

Resonance flap – this controls the resonance supercharging, a form of intake air oscillation tuning and is only active between 3120 and 5120rpm.

Secondary air pump – this electric pump injects additional air during the warm-up cycle to reduce pollutants.

Electric fans – the two-stage cooling fans are mounted in front of the radiators and are controlled by the DME. See the air conditioning section for operating conditions.

Fuel pump – this is mounted in the fuel tank, and is controlled by the DME.

Cruise control – (DME 7.x) the DME regulates the vehicle speed based on inputs from the cruise control switches, and speed sensors, etc. Note that on cars with DME 5.2.2 there is a separate cruise control actuator, which is independent of the DME.

Starter – it is the DME that signals the starter motor.

Engine compartment fan – the engine compartment fan is switched on when the engine compartment temperature is greater than 80°C or the coolant temperature is greater than 102°C.

If the ignition is switched off and the engine compartment temperature is more than 60°C, the DME monitors it for another 20 minutes. During this time, the engine compartment temperature is checked every 10 seconds. If the engine compartment temperature is greater than 85°C, the engine compartment fan is switched on for 20 seconds. If the engine compartment temperature is still greater than 85°C after this time, the fan remains on for a further 30 seconds.

So, as you can see, there is a lot going on. Essentially, the DME is reading all the inputs, calculating the required amount of fuel, ignition spark timing, throttle opening, camshaft lift and timing, etc, and instructing each actuator to do its job 3 times for every engine revolution!

Diagnostics

When the 986 Boxster and 996 911 were introduced, Porsche dealers were supplied with the Porsche System Tester 2 (PST2) for vehicle diagnostics, control module programming and module coding.

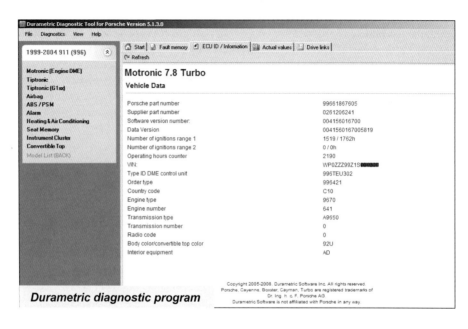

Durametric diagnostic program

This was subsequently replaced by the Porsche Integrated Workshop Information System (PIWIS) when the 987 and 997 models were introduced.

Both were based on Bosch KTS diagnostic testers, with bespoke software for Porsche models.

For all but the most ardent home

mechanic these systems are out of reach, but for proper diagnosis of faults some kind of tester is required.

DME fault codes and sensor outputs can be read by simple hand-held code readers or scanners and the Check Engine light can be extinguished with these devices once the fault has been corrected. Unfortunately, this does not apply to RoW cars with DME 5.2.2.

For more comprehensive diagnosis of the DME and many other control modules, the only viable aftermarket solution is the Durametric interface and software. This is the only 'DIY' software I am aware of which is written specifically for Porsche cars. It is available in several packages, but the Enthusiast version is ideal and affordable. It is supplied as a PC application, with a USB interface which plugs into the diagnostic port on the car.

The software will read the control unit information, display any fault codes, read out sensor values and plot them on a graph, and allow you to control and test some of the actuators and devices. It is an invaluable tool for fault finding, as without such a program you are just guessing. For more information visit www.durametric.com

Faults

Not all faults will trigger the Check Engine Light (CEL), especially on RoW cars. If the warning light flashes, ease off the accelerator and after a few seconds the light should come on solid. If the light does not stop flashing, stop the car as soon as possible, otherwise serious damage can be done to the catalytic converters.

Once the fault codes have been read, you can start on making a diagnosis. Here are some common problems:

MAF Sensor

The MAF sensor measures the air entering the throttle body. Read out the mass air flow and if necessary convert the reading to kilograms per hour. At warm idle (~700rpm) this value should be 17 kg/hr (+/-2.5). Any major deviation is a sign that it is not reading correctly. The reading should increase with engine speed, so gently open the throttle to check that the value rises accordingly. Fault codes caused by a faulty MAF will usually come in pairs – one for each cylinder bank, as both banks are affected.

A faulty MAF sensor can also bring on the PSM and ABS warnings, usually under heavy acceleration. This is because the ABS module uses data from the DME and a faulty MAF will cause implausible data to be sent from the DME to the PSM module. The reason a CEL is not illuminated (on a RoW car) is that a MAF fault will not trigger the CEL.

Oxygen Sensors

There is a sensor on the upstream side of the catalytic converter on each cylinder bank, which is used for adjusting the fuelling. The sensor after the catalytic converter is used to determine the efficiency of the cat. Read the sensor output voltages. These should fluctuate very rapidly, within the range of 0.04V to 0.79V. If the fluctuation is sluggish, it is a sign that the sensor is failing. Fault codes for oxygen sensors will normally be single codes, as a sensor fault will affect one bank only.

Misfires

The system will record misfires for each cylinder. Two common causes of misfires are:

Ignition coil packs – these present themselves as fault codes for individual cylinder(s). The coil packs are exposed to the elements under the car and the insulation can split, allowing water in and causing a short circuit or high tension tracking.

Variocam coils or solenoids – if a Variocam solenoid or coil fails, it produces misfire codes for the whole cylinder bank. This can also be caused by a bad or broken electrical connection to the coil.

A bad fuel injector will also produce an individual cylinder fault code, but this is a much rarer occurrence.

System Adaption

Over a period of time the fuelling and timing values adapt, to take into account fuel quality, etc. Many people find that resetting the adaption values to the factory defaults improves performance and driveability.

On cars with DME 5.2.2 this can be achieved by disconnecting the battery for a few minutes. On cars fitted with an alarm siren and tilt sensor (standard in the UK and Belgium) the siren will sound when the battery is disconnected. To prevent this happening, turn the ignition switch to position 1 before disconnecting the

Remove two security torx screws

negative terminal of the battery.

On cars with DME 7.2 and 7.8 the process is simpler. Simply turn on the ignition, but do not start the engine, or touch the throttle pedal. After 60 seconds, switch off the ignition for at least 10 seconds. The following criteria is required for successful adaption:
- the vehicle must be stationary
- battery voltage must be greater than 10V
- the engine temperature must be between 5°C and 100°C
- intake air temperature must exceed 10°C

Unclip the connector

MAF sensor cleaning/ replacement

Despite being publicised as being "immune to dirt", and lasting over 100,000 miles, the reality is that many need replacing at about half that distance. The life can also be affected by over-oiled aftermarket cone air filters, as oil mist can contaminate the hot film. If you are using such a filter, be very careful to follow the instructions when cleaning and re-oiling.

The MAF can benefit from an occasional clean, which may help to prolong the life by removing contaminants. The MAF is fitted to the exit tube of the filter housing on the M96 Carrera and Turbo engines.

Spray into the side opening

Spray into the bottom opening

The MAF is secured with two M5 Torx screws with T20 security heads. These have a small 'pip' in the centre to prevent the use of a standard Torx driver. Security bits are readily available from tool shops.

I find it is much easier to remove the MAF from its housing before disconnecting the plug connection. Undo the two screws and slide the sensor out of the housing.

Unclip the connector by squeezing the clips and ease the sensor from the plug. There are two different styles of clip. Earlier types have the clips on the outer edges.

Use an oil-free isopropyl alcohol aerosol spray and liberally spray into the lower side opening until it drips out.

Shake out the fluid and spray into the bottom opening, again until it drips out.

Repeat this process two or three times. Shake out any excess fluid and allow a few minutes for any fluid left in the cavity to evaporate.

Refitting is a reverse of the above. The screw holes in the MAF are offset, so it cannot be assembled the wrong way round.

Oil Pressure Sensor

On a Carrera, this is located on the right hand cylinder head, about 2/3 back in the engine compartment, pointing vertically upwards. There are two connectors on the top face, one for the warning lamp and one for the gauge pressure reading.

On a Turbo, the sender is on the oil filter housing on top of the engine, behind the filter can.

The sensors are prone to failure, resulting in the pressure gauge falling to minimum or rising to maximum. On facelift cars, this is accompanied by a warning message in the OBC, which can be alarming, to say the least.

DME data and engine over-revs

The DME stores the following information, depending on model year and specification, in the Vehicle Data section:
- Number of ignitions, range 1
- Number of ignitions, range 2
- Operating hours counter
- Vehicle Identification Number
- DME control unit ID
- Order type
- Country code
- Engine type
- Engine number
- Transmission type
- Transmission number
- Radio/PCM code

- Body colour
- Convertible top colour
- Interior equipment code
- Number of programming operations
- Navigation system code
- Total distance in km
- Option codes

This data can be read with a PST2, PIWIS, or Durametric tester, albeit that the latter has some limitations.

The most talked about value of these data is the "Number of ignitions, range X", or as people often refer to them – Type 1 and Type 2 Over-revs.

So what does this mean? Is it a sign a car has been abused? This is how the data appears on a vehicle report from a PIWIS tester:

Range 1 shows the cumulative number of ignitions when the rev-limiter was reached and the time (in engine operating hours) when it last occurred. Range 2 shows the number of ignitions when over-rev conditions have occurred and the time of the last event.

In this case, the car has done a total of 1007.2 hours and there was a case of the

Oil pressure switch - Carrera

911 (996) DME Vehicle data
Number of ignitions, range 1
   990   1002.2h
Number of ignitions, range 2
   2   900.7 h
Operating hours counter
   1007.2

Section of vehicle data report

	Range 1	Range 2
Carrera	7300-7900	7900+
Turbo	6750-7250	7250+
GT3	8200-8800	8800+

Range 1 rev limit being reached 5 hours previously, at 1002.2 hours. There are also two ignitions recorded at Range 2, some 106.5 hours ago.

A Range 1 over-rev is usually the sign of some spirited driving, when the driver has reached the rev limiter when accelerating, and causes no damage whatsoever.

A Range 2 condition can exist by (typically) a premature downshift from high engine revs, causing a true over-rev condition.

Bear in mind that these are number of ignitions. To work out the number of engine revolutions, divide by 3, as there are three ignitions per revolution of a 6-cylinder engine. Depending on the engine type and model, Range 1 and Range 2 have different values, as follows:

Therefore, you can see in this case that the duration of Range 2 over-revs was insignificant, equating to just 0.005 seconds for this car, a 996 Turbo.

Note that Tiptronic cars never record Range 2 ignitions, as the control unit will not allow a downshift that would cause an over-rev condition. *996*

Traction control and PSM

Traction Control

ABS (Antilock Braking System) version 5.3 with optional Traction Control (TC) was fitted to the 996 Carrera 2 when it was introduced. TC is a combination of ABD (Automatic Brake Differential) and ASC (Automatic Slip Control). Power reduction and individual wheel braking are used to control slippage when it is detected by the ABS sensors.

If one wheel spins faster than the other, that wheel is braked (ABD). The ABD is active at speeds below 62.5mph.

If the TC unit detects wheel slippage, it sends a signal to the DME specifying the nominal engine torque that should be applied to reduce slippage (ASC). The DME reads the actual engine torque, and if there is a deviation, it adjusts it accordingly. Because the throttle is cable operated, the DME cannot control throttle opening, so it reduces power by shutting off the fuel injectors sequentially and retarding ignition timing until the actual and

Conditions when TC can be very useful!

nominal torques are balanced.

If TC is switched off, a warning light is displayed in the instrument cluster. ABD remains active.

PSM

The optional PSM (Porsche Stability Management) is a far more comprehensive stability control system. PSM version 5.3 was introduced as an option on the 1999 Carrera 4 (coinciding with the introduction of electronic throttle) and PSM 5.7 became an option

on all models from MY2000.

A Technical Bulletin issued at the time said "PSM is an active control system for stabilising a vehicle at the limit of its driving dynamics capability. PSM includes functions such as ABS, ABD, ASR (traction-slip control), EBV (Electronic Brake-force Distribution), as well as a longitudinal dynamics control system MSR (engine drag torque control). In addition to this, the vehicle is stabilised at the limit of its driving dynamics capability within the transverse dynamics control system by FDR (driving dynamics control system)."

So what does that mean in practical terms? Well, it will give you a great deal of assistance in a tricky situation, but it won't save you if you drive beyond the limits of the car.

The system has various input sensors to detect direction, speed, yaw and lateral acceleration to determine the actual direction of the car.
● Individual wheel speed is read from the ABS sensors
● Rotation and lateral acceleration

sensors are located in the PSM control unit in the centre console.

● The steering angle sensor on the steering column measures the direction of the front wheels.

● Pressure sensors in the ABS pump measure the braking force.

● The brake light switch determines if the brakes are applied.

● The handbrake switch is monitored, to determine if it is applied.

● The CAN data bus supplies the PSM unit with accelerator position and engine torque from the DME.

In a straight line, ABS operates in the normal way, by sensing wheel lock. Braking forces to individual wheels are controlled to reduce braking distances to a minimum. ABD and ASC work as described in Traction Control, except that throttle is controlled electronically to reduce engine torque.

If braking does not provide enough control, PSM intervenes in engine management with MSR (engine drag torque control). This adjusts the ignition timing, fuel injectors and throttle angle to stabilise the car.

When all this happens mid-corner, FDR (drive dynamics control) is there to help out. This registers the direction the driver wants to take, road speed and deceleration, using a steering angle sensor and the wheel speeds.

FDR calculates the required yaw and lateral acceleration required to achieve the desired path and compares it to the actual yaw and lateral acceleration recorded by the sensors. With this information PSM intervenes by controlling the braking forces on individual wheels. If the car is understeering, it will brake the inside rear wheel to help pull it back in line. Conversely, if the car is oversteering, it will brake the front outside wheel to achieve the same effect. If braking is insufficient to stabilise the car, then MSR is initiated. When the system activates, a yellow warning triangle flashes in the instrument cluster.

If PSM is switched off, a yellow 'PSM Off' warning light appears in the cluster. Note that ABD will remain active. This light also illuminates if there is a fault in the PSM system. A yellow light also appears in the cluster if there is a fault with the ABS system.

Faults

It has to be said that major PSM faults are extremely rare. There are, however, three common issues that affect the PSM system.

As previously mentioned, a faulty MAF sensor can trigger a PSM fault. This is due to an implausible signal being sent from the DME to the PSM module. The brake light switch is a common cause of a PSM fault. Even if the brake lights are working there may still be a fault with the switch, as there are two sets of contacts inside and one set can fail without affecting the brake lights. If an ABS wheel speed sensor fails, or becomes effectively disconnected by a bad connection, this will bring on the PSM fault light.

Diagnosis of the system requires a PST2, PIWIS, or Durametric tester. Fault codes can be read and analysed, and confirmed by monitoring sensor outputs to check they are working correctly or not. 996

Transmission

Manual transmission

The completely new G96 6-speed manual transmission was developed for the 996 and manufactured for Porsche by Getrag. This gearbox is used in all models, albeit with different ratios for some variants. A limited-slip differential was available to order, option code M220.

The gear lever is connected to the gearbox by two cables that link to shift levers on the side of the transmission.

The clutch is hydraulically operated, sharing its fluid reservoir with the braking system. The Turbo models have a hydraulically assisted clutch, using the power steering pump for hydraulic pressure, but having a separate reservoir in the front compartment (see Owner Checks).

A popular modification is to fit a short-shift kit, which reduces the lever movement and gives a sportier feel. Porsche offer such a kit in their Tequipment catalogue or there are several aftermarket kits from companies such as B&M.

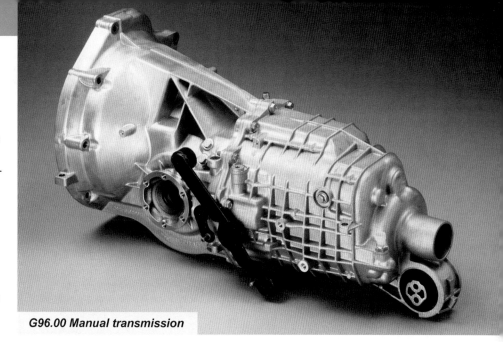

G96.00 Manual transmission

Problems

Generally speaking, the transmissions are very reliable, but the mechanical sympathy shown by the driver is a significant factor in the longevity of the clutch and gearbox. Major mechanical work is beyond the scope of this book, but there are a few things to look out for if you have trouble.

Shifting from first to second gear can tend to be a little 'notchy' when cold, but this should disappear when warm. If this persists when hot, it could be a sign that the 2nd gear synchromesh ring has become worn and requires replacement.

The shift cables are connected with plastic ball joints at the gear lever end, and these joints can break. They are available as replacement parts and are fairly easy to change yourself. A rarer failure is when the the cable becomes detached from the metal ball joint at the transmission end. This requires the cable assembly to be changed.

The cables are clipped to brackets on the side of the transmission and it is quite common for these clips to pop out or break. The result is usually that the lever becomes floppy and gears 1, 3 & 5 (or 2, 4 & 6) are lost. The clips can be replaced, but many people simply use

Manual transmission lever

a nylon cable tie around the bracket to reattach them.

It is impossible to give a mileage for the life of a clutch, but it is usual for the pedal operation to become much heavier towards the end of its life. Ultimately it will start slipping at the end of its life, at which point it is important to change it before damage is done to the flywheel. Because the Turbo clutch is hydraulically assisted, this heaviness is less obvious.

The Turbo has a hydraulic accumulator – a spherical chamber attached to the slave cylinder – which can leak internally and affect the pedal pressure. If this happens the fluid level in the clutch reservoir can go up and overflow (into the area to the right side of the battery), while the fluid in the power steering pump goes down accordingly. The accumulator is available as a separate part.

Tiptronic Transmission

5-speed Tiptronic S transmission was available as an option on all but the GT

models of the 996, option code M249.

Pre-facelift models were fitted with a transmission manufactured by ZF, based on their 5HP19 unit. For the Turbo and subsequent facelift Carreras, a transmission manufactured by Mercedes Benz, based on their 722.6 unit was adopted to cope with the additional power.

Tiptronic is far more than a power shifted automatic transmission. This gearbox has a complex controller that recognises your current driving style and selects an appropriate shift map. ZF control modules have 5 shift maps, while the MB modules have 250.

In addition, there is a warm-up map, which operates when the engine temperature is below 32°C (90°F). When this map is in operation the vehicle always starts in first gear and the shift points operate at higher engine speeds. This is to get the engine and catalytic converters up to operating temperature faster. A little-known fact is that the MB transmission has two reverse ratios, the lower one being selected for warm-up.

A96.00 Tiptronic transmission (ZF)

An Automatic Transmission Fluid (ATF)/water heat exchanger is used to cool the transmission fluid and a centrally mounted front radiator is added to the cooling system for additional cooling capacity.

On Tiptronic cars there is a limiting device preventing engine revs exceeding 4000rpm when in Neutral.

There is also a torque converter lock-up clutch, which locks the torque converter when in second gear and above, depending on the engine speed and load.

Driving in Automatic Mode

When operated in Automatic mode, the transmission has several special functions:

Prevention of up-shifting before corners – if the throttle is lifted quickly the transmission holds the current gear. If the brake is then applied, the transmission will downshift if appropriate to the conditions. When the throttle is re-applied, the shift map resumes.

Tiptronic selector and steering wheel switches

Gear retention in corners – If the system detects lateral acceleration, the respective gear is retained depending on the shift characteristic and acceleration.

Active map shifting – If the throttle pedal is depressed rapidly (but not to the kick-down position) the transmission will shift to the sportiest map. If the throttle is then closed by 25%, the map will revert to the previous one in effect.

Kick-down – If the pedal is pressed to the floor it activates the kick-down switch, which will select the lowest gear allowable for the conditions. This gear will be retained until either the rev-limiter is activated, or the throttle is reduced to 70% of full throttle.

Shift-up on slippery conditions – If the throttle is lifted under icy conditions, the engine braking effect can cause the rear wheels to slip. The system measures the difference between front and rear wheel speeds and shifts to a higher gear if slippage is detected.

Ignition suppression at gear shift – The ignition is briefly suppressed when the gear is shifted to give a smoother gear change.

On later Tiptronics (from around MY1999 onwards) operating the steering wheel switches while in Automatic mode will temporarily engage Manual mode. It will revert to Automatic mode after 8 seconds.

When the engine is warm, the transmission will start off in second gear (see warm-up map above). Pressing the accelerator sharply (but not to the point of kick-down) will cause it to shift to first gear.

Driving in Manual Mode

Sliding the selector lever to the left engages manual mode and gear selection is made using the steering wheel switches.

When the rev-limiter is reached, the gearbox will shift up automatically. If a downshift is selected when the engine speed is above that at which an over-rev condition would result, the downshift is prevented. Therefore and unlike on a manual transmission car, an over-rev condition is not allowed.

Pressing the downshift button twice quickly will shift down two gears if conditions allow. The kick-down switch on the throttle pedal is inactive in Manual mode.

In manual mode, the car will always start off in second gear, no matter how far, or quickly, the accelerator is pressed, unless first gear has been specifically selected when stopping.

Problems

Generally speaking, Tiptronic transmissions are highly reliable and major faults are rare.

If an electrical or electronic fault occurs, the transmission goes into a Limited Driving Program. The D and 4 lights in the instrument cluster flash alternately and "Tiptronic Emergency Run" appears in the OBC display on facelift cars. It is perfectly safe to drive the car if this condition occurs. It can sometimes be caused by a 'lazy' switch contact in the selector and if this is the case, switch off the engine and re-start the car. If the problem persists, seek specialist advice. A diagnostic check should reveal the problem.

Tiptronics have a "Multi-Function" switch to tell the control module the position of the gear selector. The contacts in these switches can fail, causing problems such as a harsh engagement of Drive from Neutral or an odd display of gear lights in the instrument cluster (which is confusing to the control module). On ZF gearboxes, the switch is located on the side of the transmission and on MB gearboxes at the bottom of the gear selector mechanism. Both are available as separate parts for replacement.

Problems with the brake light switch or shift lock solenoid on the selector lever can prevent the lever from moving from the P position.

ATF leaks are rare. They are probably more so on the MB transmissions. My own Turbo suffered such a leak on one of the gaskets. Unfortunately, Porsche only supply a few internal parts to the Tiptronic transmissions, preferring to supply complete exchange units.

However, specialists are able to source Mercedes parts and achieve effective repairs at a fraction of the cost.

The scheduled change period of automatic transmission fluid is 96,000 miles. A fluid change replaces less than half the total quantity, as a lot is retained in the torque converter and pipe work. Many experts recommend a more frequent change.

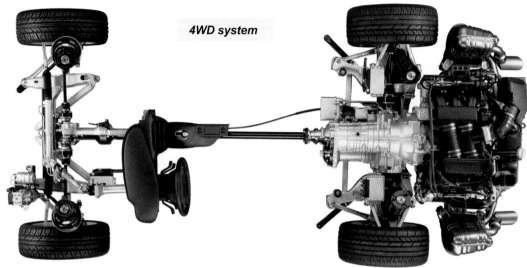

4WD system

Four Wheel Drive System

All except GT models were available with the optional 4WD system, option code M339. 4WD vehicles had PSM as standard.

The output shaft from the gearbox to the front axle contains a torque sensitive viscous coupling. Apart from transmitting the drive, this coupling compensates for any difference in speed between the front and rear wheels.

The outer plates of the coupling are attached to its casing and the inner plates are attached to the hub, with the space between them being filled with a silicone fluid.

If there is a speed difference between front and rear wheels, the frictional properties of the fluid cause the drive to be transferred from the faster rotating

plates to the slower ones.

5% of engine power is always transmitted to the front wheels, but this can increase to up to 40% in extreme conditions.

A conventional front differential transfers the drive to each front wheel. This simple but effective system is completely self-contained, having no electronic control. 996

Suspension

996 front (upper) and rear (lower) suspension systems

The 996 front suspension setup consists of a MacPherson strut with a 'wishbone' and a forked diagonal arm. At the rear is a multi-link rear axle, which Porsche call their LSA (Light, Stable, Agile) design. Each is mounted on a lightweight cast aluminium frame. Tubular anti-roll (sway) bars connect left and right hand sides using drop links.

The steering rack is mounted directly on the front frame. Tie rods connect the rack to the wheel hubs.

The steering column is in two pieces, with universal joints at the mid-point and at the steering rack end.

For the 996, the suspension was offered in 3 packages, which could be specified at the time of order. The standard package (option code M029) is, to a certain degree, a compromise between handling and comfort. For the majority of owners this is a sensible choice, particularly if road conditions are poor in your area.

The M030 sports suspension package consisted of stiffer springs, anti-roll bars and dampers. This gave a 10mm (0.4 inch) lower ride height and a much sportier feel.

The X74 package lowered the car by 30mm (1.2 inches) compared to standard. This was a much more track focussed setup and is a little extreme for daily street use.

Lower wishbone and anti-roll bar (see text for key)

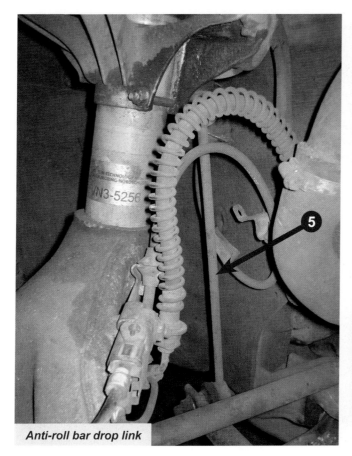

Anti-roll bar drop link

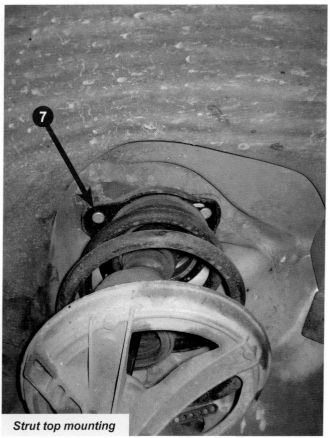

Strut top mounting

The Turbo and C4S models featured a version of the M030 package as standard (10mm lower) and the GT variants had a package similar to the X74. The Turbo and C4S were also offered with a 20mm (0.8 inch) lower suspension package, option code X73.

Problems

I would just like to add a note here about the lower suspension arm and its terminology. Technical Bulletins refer to it as the transverse arm, but it is commonly also called a 'coffin' arm (due to the shape) or a lower control arm. However, the Porsche parts program refers to it as a wishbone, so that is the term I have used, despite it not being a Y shape, as in common usage.

The 996's suspension, like all mechanical systems, is subject to wear with use. This usually manifests itself by the appearance of strange noises or a change in vehicle handling.

The type of noise can sometimes give a clue to the cause of the problem. A common noise is a creaking sound like

Badly rusted rear anti-roll bar

Forked control arm and track rod end

old bed springs. This is almost certainly a dry ball joint **(3)** or rubber bush **(2)** in the wishbone **(1)** and usually manifests itself when the car is warm.

A light rattling or clonking sound over rough surfaces, sounding like a loose board in the front compartment, is often caused by a worn joint in one of the anti-roll bar drop links. A simple way to test this is to disconnect one of the lower joints of the drop link **(5)** from the anti-roll bar **(4)**. Moving the ARB and the detached drop link by hand, you can often feel if there is play in one of the joints. The ARB mounting bushes can also wear the surface of the anti-roll bar itself.

Fairly loud clonking or cracking sounds when turning on full steering lock can often be blamed on failed rubber bushes in the strut top mountings **(7)**. The aluminium centre sleeve can become detached from the rubber bush.

Other noises can be more difficult to diagnose as they are often more intermittent and are generally similar 'clonking' sounds. The bearing ends of the forked control arms **(6)** can also wear, resulting in play, also giving a rattling sound.

Worn joints in the track rod ends (8) and inner track rod ends (on the end of the steering rack, under the rubber boot) can produce rattling or creaking noises, but these can often be reproduced by turning the steering wheel from side-to-side with the engine idling and the car on firm ground. They also tend to make the car wander, or 'tramline' on rutted roads.

The rack and pinion and bearings in the steering rack can wear, but this is extremely rare. More common problems are leaks in the hydraulic lines or cracked ferrules of the pipe joints.

At the rear, the same applies to the suspension elements. In addition to the front components of lower wishbones and forked control arms, there are two upper wishbones and a lower track rod, all of which have joints and bushes that can wear.

Repairs are usually made by fitting replacement components. There have been reports of somewhat poor quality aftermarket replacements and I would

Wheel Alignment Settings

	Carrera 2/4 M029 & M030 - USA	Carrera 2/4 M029 - RoW	Carrera 2/4 M030 - RoW	
Vehicle Height - Front				
17" Wheels	157 ± 10	147 ± 10	137 ± 10	
18" Wheels	158 ± 10	148 ± 10	138 ± 10	
Vehicle Height - Rear				
17" Wheels	157 ± 10	157 ± 10	147 ± 10	
18" Wheels	163 ± 10	163 ± 10	153 ± 10	
Alignment - Front axle				
Toe unpressed (total)	+ 5' ± 5'	+ 5' ± 5'	+ 5' ± 5'	
Toe difference angle at 20° lock	- 1° 20' ± 30'	- 1° 50' ± 30'	- 2° 20' ± 30'	
Camber (with wheels in straight-ahead position)	0° ± 15'	- 15' ± 15'	- 15' ± 15'	
max. difference, left to right	20'	20'	20'	
Caster	8° ± 30'	8° ± 30'	8° ± 30'	
max. difference, left to right	40'	40'	40'	
Alignment - Rear axle				
Toe per wheel	+ 10' ± 5'	+ 10' ± 5'	+ 10' ± 5'	
max. difference, left to right	10'	10'	10'	
Camber	- 1° 10' ± 15'	- 1° 10' ± 15'	- 1° 10' ± 15'	
max. difference, left to right	20'	20'	20'	
Anti-roll bar setting (hole position from outer end)				
Front				
Rear				

Dimensions are in millimetres. Angles are in degrees & minutes.
Front height is measured from the road surface to the underside of the 18mm A/F bolt head securing the front control arm to the body. Rear height is measured from the road surface to the location hole in the underside of the rear side section (between the toe and camber eccentrics).

Carrera 2/4 X74	Turbo & C4S USA	Turbo & C4S RoW	Turbo & C4S X73	GT2	GT3 up to MY2003	GT3 from MY2004	GT3 RS from MY2004
117 ± 10							
118 ± 10	158 ± 10	138 ± 10	128 ± 10	118 to 123	102 to 112	115 to 120	115 to 118
127 ± 10							
133 ± 10	163 ± 10	153 ± 10	133 ± 10	133 to 138	125 to 135	128 to 133	128 to 133
+ 5' ± 5'	+ 5' ± 5'	+ 5' ± 5'	+ 5' ± 5'	+ 8' ± 2'	+ 8' ± 2'	+ 8' ± 2'	+ 2' ± 2'
Carrera 2 = - 2° 20' ± 30' Carrera 4 = - 1° 40' ± 30'''	- 1° 20' ± 30'	- 1° 50' ± 30'	- 1° 50' ± 30'	- 1° 50' ± 30'	- 1° 30' ± 30'	- 1° 30' ± 30'	- 1° 30' ± 30'
- 30' ± 15'	0° ± 15'	- 30' ± 15'	- 45' ± 15'	- 1° ± 5'	- 1° ± 5'	- 1° ± 5'	- 50' ± 5'
20'	20'	20'	20'	10'	10'	10'	10'
8° ± 30'	8° ± 30'	8° ± 30'	8° ± 30'	8° ± 30'	8° ± 30'	8° ± 30'	8° ± 30'
40'	40'	40'	40'	40'	40'	40'	40'
+ 10' + 5'	+ 10' ± 5'	+ 10' ± 5'	+ 10' ± 5'	+ 13' ± 2'	+ 13' ± 2'	+ 13' ± 2'	+ 13' ± 2'
10'	10'	10'	10'	5'	5'	5'	5'
- 1° 40' ± 10'	- 1° 25' ± 15'	- 1° 25' ± 15'	- 1° 40' ± 15'	- 1° 50' ± 5'	- 1° 50' ± 5'	- 1° 50' ± 5'	- 1° 50' ± 5'
20'	15'	15'	15'	10'	10'	10'	10'
					3	4	3
					2	3	2

Alignment values should be made with a full fuel tank, with spare wheel and tools, but without driver or additional weights suggest only using genuine Porsche parts, those from the original equipment manufacturer (TRW), or a highly reputable source.

It is quite common for the rear suspension on Turbo and GT models to sag after a period of time. This is thought to be due to the extra engine weight and it can cause the car to ride with a nose-up attitude. This can be rectified with adjustment or, at worst, new rear springs.

Wheel Alignment

Over a period of time, wheel alignment can go out of adjustment. This causes several problems, such as increased and uneven tyre wear. It can also upset the handling of the car.

I would suggest having the alignment checked every two years with modern laser alignment equipment – and operated by somebody experienced at doing this job on Porsches.

Adjustment is available on all models for front and rear camber and toe. Caster angle adjustment is not normally required, but can be achieved by the fitting of a special lower wishbone. This has an eccentric bush to adjust for caster and is only fitted in exceptional circumstances.

The tables on pages 94-95 show the factory recommended settings for each model. These settings should give stable handling and even tyre wear, For a more track-focused setup it is likely you might want to go beyond these parameters.

However, subtle differences in handling can be achieved working within the standard setting range. If the car doesn't somehow quite seem to handle as you would like, a good suspension tuner should be able to advise you. Small adjustments to camber and toe can have a noticeable effect to the feel of the car. For example, I run the minimum camber settings front and rear, which I find makes the car less 'nervous' when pressing on over the bumpy roads we have in my area. The trade-off for this is slightly more understeer (push) from the front end.

Upgrades

By far the most popular upgrade for the standard Carrera is to fit the M030 sports suspension. This is available as a kit and is often offered by Porsche as a highly subsidised retrofit package. This package can be less than half the cost of the individual items. M030 is a perfect compromise for most drivers and it gives the car a much sportier feel, while also improving the appearance. In common parlance, it makes it feel much more 'planted'.

Note that the USA and RoW M029 and M030 systems are substantially different, with the RoW suspension systems being 10mm lower.

The X74 package is much more track focussed and is usually a much more expensive option. An alternative, which gives much more flexibility and adjustment, is to fit a coilover suspension kit.

Coilover kits, such as the Bilstein PSS10, or KW Variant 3, give the ability to adjust ride height and damper settings, so that the car can be set up to your specification. These kits replace the dampers, springs and usually the top mountings. 996

Brakes

The Carrera 2 and Carrera 4 models were fitted with 4-piston calipers front and rear, with cross-drilled and ventilated discs (rotors) of 318mm (12.5 inches) front and 299mm (11.77 inches) rear diameter. Calipers were finished in black on C2 models, and titanium (silver) on C4 models.

C4S, Turbo, and early GT3 models had larger (330mm, 13 inches) diameter discs, with larger 4-piston calipers at the front. All the calipers were painted red. In 2004 the GT3 and GT3RS models were upgraded to 350mm (13.78 inches) discs at the front, with 6-piston calipers.

The ultimate braking system for the 996 must surely be Porsche Ceramic Composite Brakes (PCCB). These were fitted as standard to the Turbo S and GT2, but were optional on other models and are distinctive with their yellow painted calipers. Apart from unmatched fade-free stopping power, they weigh around 50% that of cast iron discs, giving a useful reduction in unsprung weight.

Porsche never tend to 'over-servo' their braking systems, resulting in a higher

Standard Carrera caliper

pedal pressure. New 911 drivers often comment on the extra force required, but once used to it come to appreciate the increase in feel it provides.

The parking brake is a cable-operated system, acting on two 180mm (7.09 inches) drum brakes integral to the rear brake discs. The cable tension is adjusted at a turnbuckle at the rear of the handbrake lever in the centre console.

ABS is standard on all models. Early

996s were fitted with a 3-channel system (ABS 5.3) and cars with Traction Control had the 4-channel ABS/ASC 5.3 system. 3-channel systems can control individual front wheel braking, but the rear wheels are braked as a pair.

For MY2000 4-channel ABS (ABS 5.7) was introduced alongside the optional PSM system, giving control of braking on all four wheels.

The ABS hydraulic pump is located in the front compartment, adjacent to the brake servo.

Braking systems are all generally very reliable and mechanical faults are rare. However, cast iron discs can rust very badly indeed. Most often it is the inside faces of the discs that corrode and although the outside face may look perfectly serviceable, the discs will require replacement. This is most common on little-used cars and often attributed to washing the car and immediately putting it in the garage. If your car is a weekend or summer car, make sure you take it for a short drive to 'brake the discs dry' before putting it away.

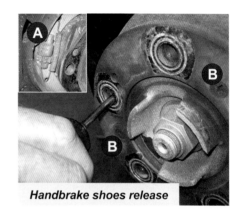

Handbrake shoes release

Note that even if the discs are badly corroded it often impossible to feel the wear through the brake pedal, even in extreme cases.

Another problem can be cracks radiating from the cross-drilled holes in the discs, caused by repeated extreme use. If any crack over 5mm appears, or reaches the outer rim, the disc should be replaced. The cross-drillings also become blocked by a build up of brake dust, so it is worth clearing them on a regular basis.

A visual inspection is usually sufficient to see if the discs require replacement

The ultimate braking system - PCCB

due to corrosion or cracking, but if the corrosion is light it is possible to have the disc surfaces ground (sometimes called skimmed), to restore a good braking surface. To determine whether a disc is suitable for this process, first the disc thickness must be measured with a micrometer to see if it is within acceptable wear limits (as it may have been ground before or the disc could already be worn out). A table of limits is shown below.

Early PCCB systems did suffer to an extent from delamination, cracking from the cross-drillings and grooves wearing in the disc surface. They are extremely expensive to replace and many owners retrofitted cast iron discs and conventional disc pads to avoid this expense.

However, development continued at a pace on PCCBs and later discs are far more durable. Since introduction there have been four design revisions of composite disc. I know of one owner who has completed well over 100,000 miles (160,000km) on the original discs and pads, and the discs still have plenty of life left in them.

Brake disc (rotor) and pad change

Raise the car off the ground, support it securely on axle stands and remove the wheels. I have found that the following method works well for me, but you may want to modify the sequence slightly or jump steps if you are changing the pads, without the discs.

Rear Axle

Turn the disc until one of the wheel bolt holes is in the horizontal position as shown (RH wheel, see opposite page). Insert a flat bladed screwdriver into the hole and work the adjuster 10-15 teeth (A) to release the handbrake shoes. Remove the two cross-headed screws (B). Note that they are offset on the hub.

Disconnect the plug for the wear

Wear sensor plug

Caliper bolt removal

'R' clip removal

Pad mounting pin

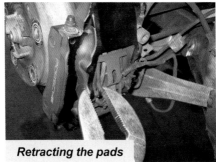

Retracting the pads

Caliper removal

Refit caliper

sensors and unclip the wire from the support bracket. Note the adjacent ABS sensor plug.

If you are changing the discs, undo the two caliper bolts. Two types are used – with either a 10mm hexagon head or Torx T55 head. Be very careful removing the bolts. The bolt holes go through the wheel carrier and are open at the other end. Water gets into the threads and can rust the ends of the bolts. The threads on the tip of the bolt can damage the wheel carrier when they are removed. Start by loosening them a ¼ turn and retighten. Then turn ¼ turn anti-clockwise and 1/8 turn clockwise. Repeat this until the bolts

become easy to turn. Remove one bolt and leave the other loosely in place until the caliper is ready to be removed.

Remove the 'R' clip that locates the pad mounting pin.

Using a pin punch, tap out the mounting pin with a hammer.

Using large water pump pliers, squeeze the pads against the caliper to push the pistons into the caliper and so give clearance between the pads and disc. Keep an eye on the level in the brake fluid reservoir, as it will go up as the pistons are retracted. Drain off a little if required.

Undo the remaining bolt, and remove the caliper. Take care not to pull

excessively on the flexible brake hose. Remove the pads by unclipping the anti-squeal pads from the caliper pistons and remove the pads, wear sensors and spring clip, all in one.

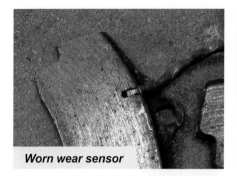
Worn wear sensor

New disc

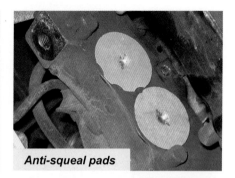
Anti-squeal pads

Refit pads and pin

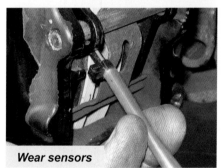
Wear sensors

Clip on the cables

If you aren't changing the discs, cut the anti-squeal pads away from the brake pads with a thin knife-edge scraper, remove the spring clips and sensors and withdraw the brake pads with the water pump pliers. Unclip and remove the anti-squeal pads.

Tie up the caliper with cord to support it.

If they are in good condition and removed with care, the wear sensors can be re-used.

Here you can see where the wear sensor has worn through, activating the warning light in the instrument cluster.

Apply a thin film of anti-seize compound

to the centering register on the wheel hub. Fit the new disc and replace the two cross-head screws (to 10Nm (7.4lb.ft) torque to be exact). Tighten the handbrake adjuster with a flat-bladed screwdriver until the disc cannot be turned. Back off the adjuster a further 4 teeth, until the handbrake shoes do not bind and again back it off a further 3-4 teeth.

Clip new anti-squeal pads into the caliper (note different sizes) and push the pistons fully back into the caliper by hand. Remove the self-adhesive backing.

Refit the caliper and tighten bolts to 85Nm (62.7lb.ft) with a torque wrench. Strictly speaking, new bolts should be used, but the bolts are not stretch bolts and if undamaged can be cleaned up and re-used. Personally, I apply some anti-seize compound to the tip of the bolt to prevent corrosion, but this is not specified in the workshop manual.

Clean up the spring clip and pin if you are re-using them, or fit new ones. Slide the pads into position and refit the clip and pin (or use new ones). Note the position of the cross-hole and tap the pin in place

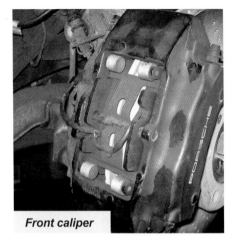

Front caliper

Brake hose bracket bolt

with a hammer and refit the 'R' clip. Press the brake pedal a couple of times to stick the anti-squeal pads to the brake pads. Check the brake fluid level.

Refit the wear sensors, or fit new ones if the old ones are damaged.

Clip the cables back in position and reconnect the sensors at the plug.

Make sure everything is in position and tightly fastened. Check the brake fluid level again and correct if necessary.

Take it easy on the first drive after fitting

new pads. Start by checking the brakes at low speed and remember it will take several miles for them to bed in properly before reaching full efficiency.

Front Axle
The principles of changing the front discs and pads are the same as for the rear, but without the obvious complication of the handbrake. However, there are a couple of other minor differences.

Here you can see that the front pads are

Front right hand disk

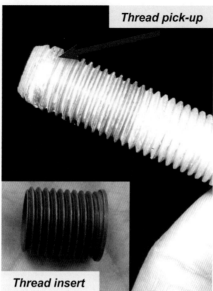

Thread pick-up

Thread insert

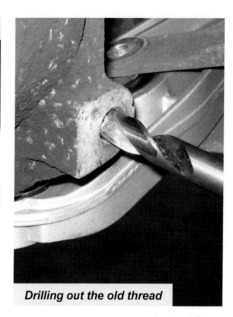

Drilling out the old thread

different, in that the pads have additional damping weights. Also, the anti-squeal pads are one-piece.

The front brake pipe has a metal pipe connecting it and the mounting bracket must be removed to allow the caliper to be removed. The bolt tightening torque is 10Nm (7.4lb.ft).

Note that the front discs are 'handed' and the cross-drillings run in lines, whereas the pattern of holes on the rear discs is symmetrical.

So, what can possibly go wrong?

As mentioned earlier, caliper bolts can rust at the tips and damage the thread in the wheel carrier when removed. An economical and effective repair is to fit a thread insert. This repair can be done with the hub carrier in place and if

properly fitted, can have equal or greater strength than the original thread.

This is the procedure for fitting a Time-Sert ® insert, which is one of the best on the market. Insert kits come with a drill bit, countersink tool, tap and fitting/sizing tool.

This is the insert (above, centre).

Brake dimensions and wear limits		C2 & C4		C4S, Turbo & GT3	
		Dimension	Wear Limit	Dimension	Wear Limit
Brake disc diameter (steel)	Front	318mm		330mm ***	
	Rear	299mm		330mm	
Brake disc diameter (PCCB)	Front			350mm	
	Rear			350mm	
Caliper pistons (steel) mm	Front	2@40 + 2@36		2@44 + 2@36	
	Rear	2@30 + 2@28		2@30 + 2@28	
Caliper pistons (PCCB) mm	Front	2@38 + 2@32 + 2@28			
	Rear	2@30 + 2@28			
Pad Thickness	Front	Approx 12.0mm	2mm	Approx 12.0mm	2mm
	Rear	Approx 10.5mm	2mm	Approx 12.0mm	2mm
Brake disc thickness (new)	Front	28mm		34mm	
	Rear	24mm		28mm	
Minimum brake disc thickness after machining	Front	26.6mm		32.6mm	
	Rear	22.6mm		26.6mm	
Brake disc wear limit	Front		26.0mm		32.0mm *
	Rear		22.0mm		26.0mm *

Counterbore tool

Tapping the new thread

Fitting/sizing tool

Brake dimensions and wear limits	C2 & C4		C4S & Turbo	
	Dimension	Wear Limit	Dimension	Wear Limit
Surface roughness of the disc after machining **	0.006mm		0.006mm	
Thickness tolerance of the brake discs, max	0.02mm		0.02mm	
Lateral runout of the brake disc, max	0.03mm		0.03mm	
Lateral runout of the wheel hub, max	0.03mm		0.03mm	
Lateral runout of the brake disc when installed, max	0.06mm		0.06mm	
Pushrod play (measured at the brake pedal plate)	Approx 1mm		Approx 1mm	
Parking brake drum diameter	180mm	181mm	180mm	181mm
Brake shoe width	25mm		25mm	
Brake pad thickness	4.5mm	2mm	4.5mm	2mm

Notes:
* PCCB disks have wear limit stamped on the disc hub.
** Peak-to-valley (Max)
*** All GT2s and MY2004 GT3 & GT3RS fitted with 350mm front discs and 6-piston calipers

Insert installation complete

Notice the shoulder on the thread end.

The damaged thread is removed by drilling with the correct size drill bit, taking great care to keep the drill straight and perpendicular to the wheel carrier.

The end of the hole is counterbored to accept the shoulder of the insert.

The new hole is tapped out with a new thread for the insert, to a depth greater than the insert length.

The insert is then fitted onto the sizing tool and wound in to the thread, until the shoulder contacts the bottom of the counterbore. Continuing to turn the tool opens out the last three threads of the insert, locking it in position.

The fitting tool is removed and you are left with a perfect new thread.

Solid inserts like these are preferred for this application, where the bolt may be removed several more times during the car's life. Coil-type inserts can unwind in this situation, causing further damage to the wheel carrier. 996

Wheels and tyres

17" Carrera wheel

18" Carrera wheel

18" Sport design wheel

The standard 996 came with 17 inch wheels, 7 and 9 inch wide (front/rear), but you could choose from plenty of optional 18 inch wheels. The option 18s came in 7.5 and 10 inch rim widths (F/R) but for the 2002MY facelift, the front wheel width was increased to 8 inches. See the data table for more information.

All 996 wheels have 5-bolt fixing on a Pitch Circle Diameter (PCD) of 130mm (5x130).

Wheels were available in the following designs:

Carrera
- 17-inch Carrera
- 17-inch Carrera II
- 17-inch Sport Classic
- 17-inch Targa
- 17-inch Cup Design
- 17-inch Carrera 4
- 17-inch Cup Design 993
- 18-inch Sport Classic II
- 18-inch Turbo Look I
- 18-inch Turbo I
- 18-inch Sport Design
- 18-inch Carrera
- 18-inch Turbo Look II

- 18-inch Sport Techno
- 18-inch GT3

Carrera 4S and Turbo
- 18-inch Turbo II
- 18-inch Turbo Look II
- 18-inch SportTechno
- 18-inch GT3

Every wheel is made from a cast aluminium alloy, painted in silver and finished in a clear coat lacquer.

Turbo II and SportTechno wheels are manufactured by a Porsche

18" Turbo II wheel

18" Turbo look I wheel

18" GT3 wheel

patented process, which results in a hollow spoke to reduce weight.

Sport Classic II and Sport Design feature a 2-piece construction. Although a smart looking design, they tend to suffer from water getting under the clear coat lacquer.

This results in unsightly corrosion of the polished surface underneath. Refurbishment of this design is usually more complex and so more expensive, and probably will need to be done by a specialist wheel restorer.

Wheel bolts

The tightening torque for securing wheels is 130 Nm (96lbft).

Wheel locking bolts are supplied as a standard fit (one per wheel) and there are a total of 30 different locking keys. Should your key become lost or damaged, Official Porsche Centres have a master key set and can match your locking wheel bolts and supply a new key.

When fitting the wheels, use the locating tool provided in the tool kit. Apart from making the job easier and safer, it helps protect the wheels and discs/rotors,

especially PCCBs.

Apply a smear of anti-seize compound (such as a Copper paste) to the bolt threads and between the bolt head and spacer. Do not apply it to the tapered face of the spacer.

Tyres

N-Rating? What's that then? Porsche work with a number of major tyre manufacturers to implement a comprehensive test program that ensures the tyre meets the required standards for handling, noise, high-speed durability and

18" Sport classic II wheel

Wheel location tool

aquaplaning, etc. Once these standards are met, the tyre goes on Porsche's Approved Tyre list and can be branded with an N specification.

N0 is assigned to the first approved version of a tyre design. Subsequent design revisions of that tyre would be branded N1, N2, N3, etc. Any completely new design of tyre would be branded N0, so there is no relationship between N ratings of tyres of different make or model.

Porsche make several recommendations about the replacement and mixing of tyres. These include:

● Only tyres of the same manufacturer, model and N rating should be mounted on the vehicle.

● When replacing worn tyres, if the appropriate N rated tyres have been discontinued, all four tyres should be replaced.

● If one tyre is damaged (cuts, bulges, puncture, etc) and the other tyre on that axle has more than 30% wear, both tyres should be replaced. This applies to all four tyres on 4WD vehicles.

Whether you decide to follow Porsche's guidance to the letter is up to you, but there are a few things you should take into consideration.

Insurance companies, particularly in the UK, can be very sensitive to 'modifications', especially in the event of a claim. Contact them and get clearance before you make any material changes to the tyres or wheels. My own insurance company was quite happy for me to use non-N rated tyres, provided they were exactly the same size, speed, and load rating.

Having a tyre on one side of the axle worn more than the other side could cause problems with PSM, as it will detect a difference in wheel speeds.

If you have a Porsche Warranty, it will be voided by the use of non-N rated tyres.

So think carefully and do your homework before making the decision!

Other tyre factors

New tyres do not offer full traction, so moderate your driving style for the first 60-100 miles.

Wheel & Tyre Sizes

Model		Size	Offset	Tyre Size	Approved Tyres
Carrera 2/4 to MY2001 - 17-inch	Front	7J x 17	RO50/55	205/50 ZR17	1, 2, 3, 4
	Rear	9J x 17	RO55	255/40 ZR17	1, 2, 3, 4
Carrera 2/4 to MY2001 - 18-inch	Front	7.5J x 18	RO50	225/40 ZR18	3, 5, 6
	Rear	10J x 18	RO65	265/35 ZR18	3, 5, 6
Carrera 2/4 Fr MY2002 - 18-inch	Front	8J x 18	RO50/52	225/40 ZR18	3, 4, 5, 6
	Rear	10J x 18	RO65	285/30 ZR18	3, 4, 5, 6
Carrera 4S and Turbo	Front	8Jx18	RO50	225/40 ZR18	3, 4, 5, 6
	Rear	11Jx18	RO45	295/30 ZR18	3, 4, 5, 6
GT2	Front	8.5Jx18	RO40	235/40 ZR18	7, 8, 9, 10, 11, 12
	Rear	12Jx18	RO45	315/30 ZR18	7, 8, 9, 10, 11, 12
GT3 (MY00-01)	Front	8J x 18	RO52	225/40 ZR18	3, 4, 5, 6
	Rear	10J x 18	RO65	285/30 ZR18	3, 4, 5, 6
GT3/RS (MY03-05)	Front	8.5Jx18	RO40	235/40 ZR18	7, 8, 12, 13
	Rear	11Jx18	RO63	295/30 ZR18	7, 8, 12, 13

Porsche Approved N Rated Tyres

1	Pirelli P Zero Rosso	N3
2	Bridgestone Potenza S-02A	N4
3	Continental ContiSportContact2	N2
4	Michelin Pilot Sport PS2	N3
5	Pirelli P Zero Rosso	N4
6	Bridgestone Potenza S-02A	N3
7	Michelin Pilot Sport 2	N4
8	Michelin Pilot Sport 2	N2
9	Michelin Pilot Sport	N0
10	Pirelli P Zero Rosso Asimmetrico	N0
11	Pirelli P Zero Rosso	N5
12	Pirelli P Zero Corsa	N4
13	Pirelli P Zero Rosso	N6

Tyres age, become brittle and crack, so Porsche recommend that tyres over 6 years old should be replaced. You can check the manufacturing date of the tyre by looking at the DOT number branded on the side wall. It is in the format WWYY, showing the week number and year.

Porsche advice is to mount winter tyres at temperatures below 7°C/45°F, because the driving characteristics of summer tyres are reduced at low temperatures.

The tyre pressures specified apply only to Porsche Approved N-Rated tyres and are specified for cold tyres (approx. 20°C/68°F).

If you are using metal valve caps, wipe a smear of anti-seize compound onto the valve threads before replacing the caps to prevent corrosion of dissimilar metals.

A table of wheel data and current N rated tyres is shown above. 996

Tyre pressures

17-inch road wheels	Front	2.5 bar (36 psi)
	Rear	2.5 bar (36 psi)
18-inch road wheels	Front	2.5 bar (36 psi)
	Rear	3.0 bar (44 psi)
Spare wheel (C2)	Front & Rear	4.2 bar (60 psi)
Collapsible emergency wheel (C4/C4S)	165/70-16	2.5 bar (36 psi)
	185/60-17	2.8 bar (41 psi)

Air conditioning was an option on the 996, but it is extremely rare to find a car without it. Manual heating systems had three rotary controls in a panel in the upper centre console to control temperature, blower speed and air distribution. There was also a button to operate the fresh air/recirculation air flap.

The air conditioning control unit and display panel was derived from an Audi part and gave full climate control.

The compressor is mounted on the top of the engine and is driven through a magnetic clutch from the polyrib drive belt. Refrigerant is pumped through pipes running down the right hand side of the car, on the underside of the floor pan, to a circuit incorporating the evaporator, a filter/dryer and two condensers, one in front of each front wheel.

The condensers are mounted directly in front of the coolant radiators and air from the front bumper inlets is ducted to flow through them. 2-speed fans are mounted behind the radiators to provide additional air flow.

The evaporator is located within the

Climate control panel. Yes, they all say 'Manuell' in manual mode!

Interior temp sensor with fan behind

main housing behind the dash, which also contains the blower fan, the inlet air (pollen) filter and temperature sensors for the inlet and outlet air. There is also a sun sensor in the centre of the dash and an interior temperature sensor on the passenger side air vent housing. Various flaps within the housing control the air flow distribution to the cabin. The heater matrix is also contained within the main housing to provide heated air.

The outside air temperature is also monitored by a sensor in the right hand air inlet in the front bumper.

The system uses industry standard R134a refrigerant (900g) with 195cc of ND8 refrigerant oil.

Problems

The most common problem with air conditioning systems on these cars are corroded and leaking condensers and pipe leaks – mainly in the area where they run under the right hand sill (rocker panel). Pipe damage is often caused by careless jack or garage ramp positioning, as the pipes run very close to the front jacking point. Pipes can also pinhole after a long period of time from fretting or rubbing on the plastic clips that hold them to the underside of the body.

When the air conditioning is switched on, it engages the magnetic clutch to start the compressor. With the engine compartment open, you will hear a clicking sound and the DME will also increase the engine idle speed. If the refrigerant pressure is low, the system will not engage the clutch, so this is a good indication of a leak. If the refrigerant charge is low, but not too low to prevent operation, it will often cause the compressor to run noisily, which is an early warning sound that matters require attention.

There is little to stop road debris from building up in the front inlets and this area should be cleaned regularly, using a crevis (long nose) tool on a vacuum cleaner. Leaves and twigs in particular turn into a soft mulch, which remains wet and provides a perfect environment for corrosion of the condensers and

radiators. You will be amazed at what gets stuck in there. As shown previously, the front bumper can be removed relatively easily and the condensers and radiators separated to remove the debris sandwiched between them.

While you have the bumper removed, a popular modification is to fit mesh grilles to the inlets, to prevent the debris from entering the inlets in the first place. There are several aftermarket kits available now, but it is a straightforward job to do it yourself. Make cardboard templates of the rear sides of the openings, cut the mesh to size, and secure in place with self-tapping screws into the black opening surrounds, or stick in place with a black

silicone mastic or hot glue gun.

The switch-on conditions for coolant/condenser blower motors are as follows:

Stage 1 (low speed) is switched on when:
a) the coolant temperature is greater than 100°C (212°F) or
b) there is an A/C demand, the intake air temperature is greater than 8°C (46°F) and the ignition is switched on.
Stage 2 is switched on when:
a) the coolant temperature is greater than 105°C (221°F) or
b) the refrigerant pressure is greater than 16 bar (232psi).

The low speed is regulated by a large resistor, fixed on the framework at the underside of the bumper. After time, these resistors fail, with the result that the fans will only run at high speed.

The pollen filter is located on the passenger side of the front compartment, under a plastic cover that is retained by a single T20 Torx screw. It is a simple matter to remove the panel and unclip the filter to replace it. 996

Mesh inlet grilles. Note outside air temp sensor

Pollen filter (RHD car shown)

Electrical systems

There are many elements to the electrical system on a 996. Some are basic switch-operated systems, whereas others are controlled by programmable control modules. It also depends on the level of equipment, as to the method of control. For example, standard seats are purely hard-wired but if you have electric memory seats, they have a control module which links to the alarm system and door mirrors. Here is an outline of the various systems on the car:

Hard-wired systems:
- Lighting
- Windows
- Wipers
- Seats
- Sunroof

Module-controlled systems:
- DME
- Tiptronic
- ABS/TC/PSM
- Air Conditioning
- Alarm System
- Airbag
- Instrument Cluster
- PCM
- Seat Memory
- Park Assistant
- Convertible Top
- Roll-over Protection
- HBA (Litronics)

Let's start with the basics – fuses and relays.

Fuses

The fuse panel is located behind a plastic cover in the driver's side footwell. The cover unclips from the top and is held by two plastic prongs in the bottom. Insert a finger into the top hole and unclip it and lift it off the prongs. In the back of the cover you should have a paper chart of the fuses and their location.

The fuse panel is lined up in columns designated 1-10 and rows A-E. Below row E you will see a yellow fuse-pulling tool and spare fuses. Depending on the model and year, you may also see a red pull-out emergency connection (see 'Emergencies') and the manual spoiler activation switch.

Fuse panel with paper fuse chart in the back of the cover

Fuses

Part No.	Colour	Amp
999.607.004.00	Lt. Brown	5
999.607.005.00	Brown	7.5
999.607.007.00	Blue	15
999.607.009.00	White	25
999.607.010.00	Green	30
999.607.017.00	Orange	40

There are differences in the locations of many fuses, depending on model, year and equipment, but there are some common to all models so the following table may be enough to get you out of trouble if the paper chart has been lost.

Fuses are readily available standard ¼" blade type but should you want to buy them from a Porsche Centre, the part numbers are as shown above.

Fuses can age, but they usually blow for a reason, so do some investigation before replacing them.

Relays and bridge plugs

There are two relay boards. One is located in the driver's footwell, above the fuse panel and the other is under

Fuses

Where used	Location	Rating	Notes
High Beam Right	A1	15A	MY1998 – 7.5A
High Beam Left	A2	15A	MY1998 – 7.5A
Low Beam Right	A9	15A	MY1998 – 7.5A
Low Beam Left	A10	15A	MY1998 – 7.5A
Fog Light, Rear Fog Light	A7	25A	
Side Marker Right	A3	7.5A	
Side Marker Left	A4	7.5A	
Licence Plate Lights, Instrument Lights	A5	15A	
Licence Plate Lights, Canada	A8	7.5A	
Reversing Lights, Mirror Adjustment	B5	7.5A	
Brake Lights, Cruise Control	B7	15A	
Turn Signal Lights	B6	15A	
Wipers	C6	25A	
Headlight Washers	C9	25A	
Power Windows Front	D1	30A	
Power Windows Rear	D4	30A	
Horns	B3	25A	
Heated Rear Window and Door Mirrors	D2	30A	
Engine Electrics	C1	25A	
Ignition. Injection, O2 Sensor Heaters	C2	30A	
Fuel Pump	C4	30A	
Radiator Fan Right	C8	30A	40A from MY2002
Radiator Fan Left	C10	30A	40A from MY2002
Engine Compartment Fan	B4	15A	
Heating & Air Conditioning	D6	30A	
Air Conditioning Control Module	E7	7.5A	

the carpet panel behind the rear seats. On a cabriolet, it is located behind the removable panel behind the rear seats.

Relay Support 1 has a series of 'bridge plugs' along the bottom edge and left hand side, which house link wires to devices with common source signals. These vary a little by model and year, but there are some useful connection points for aftermarket equipment such as radios and satellite navigation systems.

Relay Support 2 houses relays related to the rear of the car and engine compartment. Positions 6 and 12 are occupied by bridge plugs and a fuse for the Secondary Air Fan is clipped to the lower edge of the relay support.

Note that on relay Support 2, a reversing light signal is available from one of the bridge plugs in position 6, with Black/Blue wire connections. This can also be a useful connection for aftermarket devices.

Lighting

Changing bulbs is outlined in the Driver's Manual, but here are a few tips that might

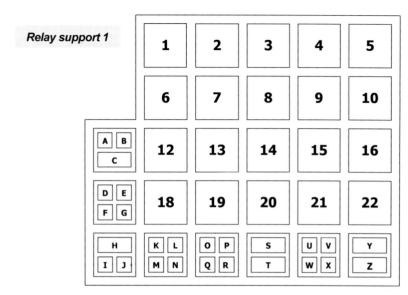

Relay support 1

Common Bridge Plugs

Location	Number	Function	Wire Colour
A or A&B	BS 16/1	Term. 15 (Ignition switched)	Black/Brown
C	BS 15	Term. 58d (Switch Lighting)	Grey/Blue/Red
E	BS 14/2	Brake Lights (Ignition switched)	Black
G	BS 13/1	Term 86s (Key in ignition switched)	Orange
H	BS 1/1	Speedometer A	Grey/Pink
R	BS 6/1	Parking Brake Signal	Brown/Yellow
Y & Z	BS 11 & 12	Term 31. (Earth)	Brown

Relay Support 1

Position	Function	Notes
1 & 2	Not used	
3	Flasher	
4	Rear Window & Mirror Heaters	
5	Trunk Entrapment (USA)/Telephone Changeover	
6 & 7	Daytime Running Lights (USA)	Double Relay
8	Headlamp Washers	
9	Terminal XE	
10	Horns	
12	Fog Lights (USA/Japan)	
13	Fuel Pump	
14 & 15	Not Used	
16	Intermittent Wiper Control	
18	Heating	
19	Radiator Fan Left, Stage 1	
20	Radiator Fan Left, Stage 2	
21	Radiator Fan Right, Stage 1	
22	Radiator Fan Right, Stage 2	
If a PSE is fitted, it will be in one of the unused positions		

Relay Support 2

Position	Function
1	DI+MFI
2	Ignition/O2 Sensor Heating
3	Spoiler Up
4	Air Conditioning Compressor
5	Changeover Relay for Cabriolet Heated Rear Screen
7	Start Lock
8	Engine Compartment Fan
9	Spoiler Down
10	Secondary Air Pump
11	Not Used
Maxi Fuse 40A – Part No: 999.607.073.00 for Secondary Air Pump	

1	2	3	4	5	6
7	8	9	10	11	12

Relay support 2

make the process a little easier.

The box wrench included in the tool kit can be a little fragile and is prone to cracking or rounding if used a lot. Preserve it for when you need it in emergencies and use a standard 5mm hexagon socket when working at home.

Don't be too alarmed by a loud 'crack' when the locking bar releases from the catch, which is quite normal.

Before re-fitting, check that the connector plug (1, upper left photo on

Headlight mounting tray

Headlight removal

Rear light unit

Light unit is held in a slot at front

Side marker lights

Interior lights

Bulb Chart

Lamp	Shape	Output
High beam headlight, dipped beam headlight (Bi-Xenon headlight as from MY2002)	D2S	35 W
Auxiliary high beam headlight (Bi-Xenon headlight as from MY2002)	H11	55 W
High beam	H7	55 W
High beam headlight as from MY2002	H9	65 W
Dipped beam headlight (Litronic headlight up to MY2001)	D2S	35 W
Dipped beam headlight	H7	55 W
Fog light	H7	55 W
Fog light as from MY2002	H3	55 W
Front parking light (Litronic, Bi-Xenon headlight as from MY2002)	H	6 W
Front parking light (up to MY2001)	W	5 W
Direction indicator, front and rear	PY	21 W
Direction indicator (USA)	MSCD40	
Direction indicator, side (MY1998 and USA)	W	5 W
Direction indicator, side (as from MY1999)	WY	5 W
Rear fog light	P	21 W
Reversing light	P	21 W
Brake light/tail light	P	21 W
Tail light (C4S, Turbo)	P	5 W
Tail light	R	5 W
Additional brake light	W	3 W
Number plate light	C	5 W
Luggage compartment/engine compartment light, interior light	K	10 W
Reading light	Xenon	6W
Door lock/exit light	W	5 W

p116) is clipped into the bracket of the headlight mounting tray. They have a nasty habit of becoming detached, which results in a poor connection between the plug and the headlamp socket. When re-inserting the headlamp unit, engage the pins of the headlight unit into the slots (2 & 3) and slide the headlamp back into position before turning the locking bar.

Note the three covers in the mid upper photo, which cover the headlamp adjusters. Cover A is for the headlight lateral adjuster. B is for headlight height and C is for foglight height. A long (150mm) 5mm ball-ended hexagon driver is required to make adjustments.

The rear lights are held in position by two button head socket cap screws and a 3mm hex key or driver is required to remove them.

When replacing the light, engage the light unit in the slot at the front and slide it home before refitting the screws.

Be careful not to over-tighten the screws, as the mounting lugs are easily broken.

The side marker lights simply unclip from the rear edge and no tools are required.

The interior light unit unclips from the front edge and has locating tags in the back edge.

The door lights unclip from their rear edge and can be removed without tools.

Problems

Ignition switches can be problematic, as after a long period of time the switch can break up inside. This usually manifests itself by the key not springing back to the off position and can make it difficult to remove. The switch is mounted on the back of the lock barrel and contains the return spring for the key and lock.

Porsche redesigned the ignition lock, which involves changing the complete lock barrel in order to fix the problem. However, the original switch is still available from VW/Audi dealers. It has the same part number as the Porsche item (4A0 905 849B). Beware of cheap imitations, as they can be very poor quality.

Another switch that is prone to failure is the main headlight switch. Again, these can break up inside and cause one or more of the lighting circuits to fail.

Electronics

Most other systems in the car are controlled by electronic control modules. The DME, Tiptronic, ABS/PSM and air conditioning modules have been covered previously. What follows is an overview of the other systems, along with common problems.

Airbags/POSIP

Early 996s had front driver and passenger airbags, but for MY1999 the POSIP (Porsche Side Impact Protection) system was introduced, adding an airbag in each front door. For MY2002 pyrotechnic seat belt tensioners combined with belt-force limiters were introduced, also controlled by the airbag module.

If the airbag warning light in the instrument cluster comes on after the initial test period at startup, diagnosis is required to establish the fault. The triggering module detects frontal impact, sensors in the door sills detect side impact, and the appropriate airbags and seat belt pre-tensioners are deployed. In the case of a rear impact, only the seatbelt pre-tensioners are activated.

The triggering unit, fixed to the floor behind the lower centre console, must be replaced after 3 activations of the system.

If working on the car involves removing or disconnecting an airbag or seat belt unit, disconnect the battery a few minutes before unplugging the device and do not reconnect until the device is plugged back in. Failure to do so will cause the airbag warning light to illuminate, which must be reset using a Porsche tester.

Park Assistant

Optional Park Assistant has a system of four ultrasonic sensors in the rear bumper, which detect the distance from nearby objects when reverse gear is engaged. A 0.5 second high pitch tone is issued from a loudspeaker in the instrument cluster when the system is activated. A continuous low pitch tone indicates a fault in the system. The fault may be simply dirt on the sensors, or a malfunction of the system which requires diagnosis.

Each sensor emits an ultrasonic beam with a horizontal beam width of approx.

120° and a vertical beam width of approx. 60°. The sensor also acts as a receiver, measuring the time taken for the sound reflection, thereby calculating the distance. Reflections are also measured by adjacent sensors to triangulate the area in between. The gap between warning tones reduces as an object is approached, becoming continuous when the distance reaches 30cm.

However, the system has limitations. Sound-absorbent obstacles (such as snow) or sound-reflecting obstacles (glass surfaces, flat painted surfaces) have an effect on the reflection behaviour of the system. Very thin obstacles or obstacles with very small reflective surfaces cannot be detected. Very low obstacles are at best indicated by an intermittent acoustic signal.

The control unit for the system is located under the left hand seat. In most cases of a fault, diagnosis is usually required, but in the case of the system becoming non-operational the cause can simply be that the reversing light switch has failed. If the reversing lights don't work, nor will Park Assistant.

Alarm system

All 996s are equipped with an alarm and immobiliser system which can be remote controlled from the key head transmitter. UK and Belgian cars were also fitted with a tilt sensor and siren as standard, to meet insurance requirements. This was an option on vehicles in other countries.

The alarm control module is located under the left hand seat. Note that this is the lowest point of the floor pan, so any water leaks gravitate to this point, and can ruin the module.

The keys have 3 basic elements. The blade, a radio remote control transmitter, and an immobiliser pill. Replacement key blades can be ordered from Porsche dealers, and are cut to the stipulated lock number which is stored on Porsche's IPAS system. Remote transmitters and immobiliser pill codes are programmed into the control unit using a PST2 or PIWIS tester, but the IPAS security codes are required.

The control module can be programmed with up to four keys. Each key register is programmed with the remote and pill codes. These registers are also used by the seat memory module (if fitted) to recognise which driver is operating the system, setting the seat and mirror positions accordingly.

Key heads are supplied with a 24-digit bar code for the radio remote and an un-programmed immobiliser pill. 'Service' (non-remote) key heads are also available which just contain the pill.

During programming, the 24-digit code is entered for the system to recognise the remote signals. The code from the immobiliser pill is read by a transponder coil and signal converter adjacent to the ignition switch. This code is entered in the key register, and the control module also writes a secret code back to the transponder pill itself.

Once a pill has been programmed to a car, it cannot be used on another car. The radio remote, on the other hand, can be programmed to another vehicle, provided the 24-digit code is known. Therefore, be aware of this if you are considering purchase of a used key on a well-known online auction site!

Another point to note is that the DME and alarm control module are programmed with a common immobiliser code number. The two codes must match in order for the engine to start. The alarm control module can only be programmed with an immobiliser code once and cannot be changed, so it cannot be transferred to another vehicle unless the appropriate code for the DME is known.

When the immobiliser is activated, it inhibits cranking, ignition and the fuel pump, to prevent the engine from being started.

Other elements of the system, depending on model and year, include:
● Motorised door locks
● Front and rear lid actuators
● Internal central locking button
● Front and rear lid microswitches
● Radio/PCM alarm contact
● Alarm horn
● Tilt sensor and alarm siren
● Alarm readiness light on dashboard
● Glove compartment microswitch
● Ultrasonic passenger compartment monitoring sensor
● Microswitches for both door lock modules
● Microswitches for door handles
● Open button for front and rear lids
● Microswitch for oddments tray
● Antenna lead for radio remote
● Fuel flap lock

Locking conditions and warnings:

When the doors are single-locked (single press of the remote button or single turn of the key in the door lock), the system is full armed. The operation should be silent, and the indicators will flash twice.

Double-locking (two quick presses of the remote button or two quick turns of the key) arms the system, but disables the interior monitoring sensor. The indicator lights will illuminate for two seconds, and the alarm horn will beep once.

On locking, the red LED in the centre of the dash will rapid flash for a few seconds,

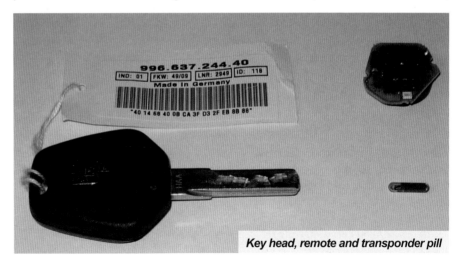

Key head, remote and transponder pill

and then settle to a single flash every 2 seconds.

Unlocking is silent, with a single flash from the indicator lights.

The vehicle can also be locked and unlocked from the button on the dash 'horseshoe' when inside the car. If the car is locked with the remote, it cannot be unlocked with the button.

If the system single-beeps on normal locking, it indicates that a compartment lid is open (usually the centre console lid). If there is a double beep (accompanied by a double flash of the dash LED every 2 seconds, this indicates an alarm system fault.

In the event of a fault that prevents remote locking of the car, you can use the emergency locking procedure to secure the vehicle until the fault is rectified. Using the door lock, turn the key to the lock position and back three times in quick succession. You may also be able to lock it by pressing the key remote locking button 3 times.

When unlocking the car with the key, the ignition must be switched on within 10 seconds or the alarm will sound.

If the car is not unlocked with the remote control for a period of 5 days the car goes into energy saving mode and the remote control is disabled. In this case, turn the key to the unlock position, but do not open the door. Press the remote locking button once and the remote control will be re-activated.

The Carrera 98 Security System fitted to all C16 UK 996s between October 1997 and 2005 has Thatcham Catagory 1 Approval. The Approval Number is TC2-900/1197.

Automatic re-locking occurs after 60 seconds if the car is unlocked by remote, but no doors are opened. This time can be set to 4-120 seconds using a Porsche tester.

The alarm module can be programmed to auto-lock the doors when switching on the ignition, or when reaching a speed of 3-6mph. A third option is available, whereby they are locked when switching on the ignition, but if opened will re-lock at 3-6mph.

Apart from programming the auto-

locking and relocking functions, there aren't any modifications that can easily be integrated into the system. However, for pure indulgence there is the Design Key. Based on the key of the Carrera GT, this is a two-button bare key head, into which the key blade, remote transmitter, and immobiliser pill are transferred from an existing key.

Cash per kilo, it is probably the most expensive piece of Porsche plastic I have ever purchased, but it was worth it for the feel-good factor alone! The part number is 000.044.000.83.

Problems

As you can see the system is quite complicated and there are several areas that cause common problems.

Key remotes

Key radio remotes can stop functioning for no apparent reason. Under normal operation the red LED on the key should flash rapidly when the button is pressed. If it does not flash, or stays on solid, the first step is to replace the battery.

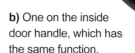

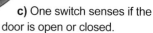

Design key

The key head is split around the centre line, and the top part (with the buttons) can be prised off from the joint near the key blade. Lift out the remote and replace the battery with a fresh CR2032 coin cell, positive terminal upwards.

If the remote still fails to work, you can restart the processor. Remove the battery and wait at least 10 seconds. Re-insert the battery with the polarity reversed (negative terminal upwards) for approximately 3 seconds. Remove the battery and re-insert with the correct polarity.

Door microswitches

There are seven microswitches in each door that control the alarm system. Two are separate switches:
a) One on the outside door handle. This switch is used to sense that the handle is lifted.

b) One on the inside door handle, which has the same function.

When the car is unlocked and either handle is lifted, this signals the alarm control module to lower the appropriate window by 10mm and turn on the interior lights. As soon as the door opens, another switch inside the door lock tells the module that the door is open, which holds the window down until the door is closed. At this point the window is raised and the dimming timer on the interior lights is started. Once the car is locked, the outside handle switches are ignored by the module.

The remaining five switches are inside the door lock assembly.

c) One switch senses if the door is open or closed.
d) One senses that the key has been turned to the 'lock' position.
e) Another senses that the key has been turned to the 'unlock' position.
f) One senses that the door lock motor has reached the 'lock' position.
g) Another senses that the door lock motor has reached the 'unlock' position.

Typical microswitch faults

All these microswitches can be problematic and it is common for one or more to fail at some time. These are some of the common failures and symptoms:
1) The door window won't drop when

lifting a handle. This is usually the handle microswitch which has failed.

2) The window drops, but goes back up when the door opens. This can be the handle microswitch or more likely the 'door open/closed microswitch' (c) has stuck. Because the system thinks the door is still closed, it sends the window back up.

3) Door window won't go up the last 10mm. This is likely to be the 'door open/closed microswitch' (c) stuck in the opposite sense to (2). The system thinks the door is still open, so won't allow the window to go back up. Note that in this case the door will still lock, but you may get a single-beep from the alarm horn.

4) Door will not lock with key. The 'key lock' microswitch (d) is broken. This is very rare, as this microswitch is hardly ever used – most times the car is locked by remote.

5) Door will not unlock with key. The 'key lock' microswitch (e) is broken. This is also very rare, for the same reason.

6) Door locks, and then immediately unlocks, usually accompanied by a

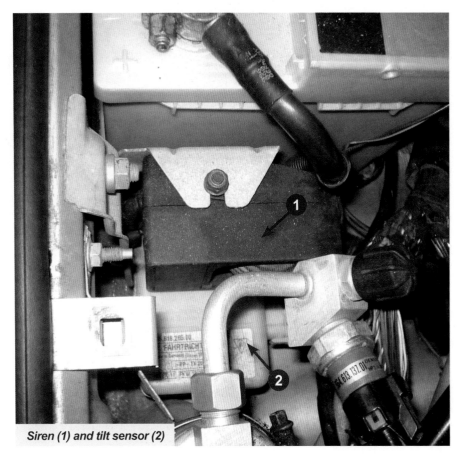

Siren (1) and tilt sensor (2)

double-beep from the alarm horn. This is the 'door locked' microswitch (f). The locking motor physically operates the door lock, but the microswitch to sense this has failed/stuck. The control module promptly unlocks the car. In this case, the only way to lock the door is to use the emergency locking procedure described earlier.

7) The door unlocks, but there is a beep from the alarm horn. This is the 'door unlocked' microswitch (g). Although the door is unlocked, the module has not recognised that. The alarm will not sound, as turning the key in the lock has deactivated it.

The inside and outside handle microswitches are available separately and are not too expensive. Although alternative equivalent switches may be available, the genuine Porsche switch comes with a connector and wiring, so it makes sense to use an original part.

The door lock microswitches are not available separately. You have to buy the complete door lock assembly, although it has been known for people to strip down the door lock and make a repair to the

Alarm horn

offending switch.

Another reason for the doors to not lock or unlock with the key can be an incorrectly fitted door lock assembly. The key barrel on the door has a blade on the back which engages in the door lock. When replacing the lock it is important to engage the blade, but this can often be overlooked. The result is that when the car is left for 5 days, the load shut-off disables the remote function and the door cannot be opened.

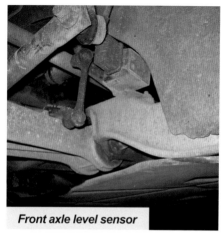

Front axle level sensor

Alarm siren & tilt sensor

The alarm siren is fitted to a bracket to the right hand side of the battery (as you look at it). Prior to MY2002, the tilt sensor was mounted directly below the siren. It is fairly common for the tilt sensors to fill with water over a long period of time, resulting in unexplained false alarms. Later cars sensibly had the tilt sensor moved to the inside of the car, under the left hand seat.

The alarm horn, fitted to all models, is on the other side of the battery, and is generally free of problems.

As with all systems utilising a control module, diagnosis with a Porsche tester is necessary to establish where the fault lies.

Headlight beam alignment (Litronic)

Automatic level control of the Litronic or Bi-Xenon headlights is controlled by a module located on the passenger side, below the airbag unit.

Sensors, located on the front and rear suspension, on the left hand side, send signals to the module, giving the level of the car at the front and back. Using this information, the module controls a stepper motor in each light to set the beam level, depending on the attitude of the car. Note that this level control is making adjustments from the height at which the headlights are set with the mechanical adjusters.

When the ignition is switched on, the lights will move down to their lowest level and then return to the normal running position. If the beams do not move to the low position, there is a fault in the stepper

motor circuit. A fault in the level sensor circuit will cause the lights to stay in the low position.

Following work on the headlight system, such as the replacement of the control module, sensors or motors, the system should be recalibrated with a PST2 or PIWIS tester.

The system itself is very reliable, but a common failure is the plastic attachment bracket of the link rod and the ball joints of the link rod itself. Both items are inexpensive and easy to replace.

Seat memory buttons

Seat Memory

The control module for the seat memory functions is located on the underside of the driver's seat. Buttons for selecting and storing memory positions are on the sill panel on the driver's side.

The system can store and recall the following positions:
- Seat adjustment front to back
- Seat front height adjustment
- Seat rear height adjustment
- Backrest adjustment
- Lumbar support
- Right and left door mirror

Memories can be set for two drivers using the memory buttons, plus memories for each key programmed to the alarm system.

To set the memories using the buttons, switch on the ignition, select reverse gear and adjust the desired positions of the seat and door mirrors. Press and hold the 'M' button and press button '1' or '2'. The positions are now stored. To recall the memory positions, switch on the ignition, or open the door, and press and hold button '1' or '2' until the seat position has been reached.

To set the memory positions for an individual key, switch on the ignition with that key and select reverse gear. Adjust the seat and door mirrors as required. Press and hold the 'M' button and then press the 'key' button (the one with the key logo). The memory positions are now stored. To recall the key memory position, unlock the car with the remote control and the seat positions will be set automatically. If the key was used to unlock the car by the door lock, switch on the ignition and press the 'key' button.

The seat position assigned to any key can be cleared from memory by switching the ignition on with that key, and pressing and holding the 'key' and '2' buttons simultaneously for at least 5 seconds.

You can interrupt the seat adjustment by pressing the central locking button or any one of the four sill buttons.

Convertible Top

The control module, located behind the panel behind the rear seats, controls the hydraulic pump to open and close the convertible top.

Hydraulic pump showing filler plug

Elements of the system include:
- Rocker switch on the dashboard 'horseshoe'
- Warning light in instrument cluster
- Microswitch on windscreen frame latching hook
- Microswitch in convertible top latch lock
- Potentiometer on convertible top mechanism (to measure roof position)
- Microswitch on convertible top mechanism
- Potentiometer on convertible top compartment lid (to measure 'clamshell' position)
- Microswitches on left and right rear section flaps (up and down)

Each step of the opening/closing process is performed in sequence and can only proceed if the previous step was completed successfully. The control module monitors each step and if a step is not confirmed within a specific time, the actuation of the drive motor is interrupted.

From MY2003 the convertible top was operable on the move, at speeds up to 30mph, but previous models had to be stationary with the handbrake applied.

Operation of the top is by the button on the dashboard, or holding the key in the door 'lock' or 'unlock' positions. Depending on model year and country-specific regulations, comfort open and closure may also be available via the key radio remote.

Diagnosis and calibration is made with the PST2 or PIWIS tester. The convertible top should be recalibrated after working on the top mechanism or hydraulics, or after emergency operation.

Most problems are with the mechanical elements of the system – typically items such as broken flaps or hinges.

Low levels of hydraulic fluid also prevent the top from opening correctly. The semi-transparent fluid reservoir is located on the bottom of the hydraulic pump, behind the panel behind the rear seats. There is a filler plug with a 5mm hexagon key hole between the two pipe unions on the front of the unit. Use a small syringe and tube to add fluid, filling it to the maximum mark on the reservoir. The system is self-bleeding, so operate the top three or four times, check the

level again and top up if necessary.

A popular modification is to install a SmartTop control module. This aftermarket device provides opening on-the-move for earlier cars and operation via the key remote on all vehicles.

Roll-Over Protection System

Apart from having strengthened 'A' pillars, the cabriolet models also have a roll-over protection system to provide additional passenger safety. This system consists of two protection hoops which are spring-ejected from a framework behind the rear seats in the event of a potential roll-over situation.

The control module is located under the carpet, between the rear seats. The module monitors acceleration, g-forces, and inclination angle. When activated, the hoops are ejected through plastic covers behind the rear seats within a few milliseconds.

Diagnosis is again with a Porsche tester, but problems with this system are exceptionally rare. Testing of the system is included in the Additional Maintenance schedule every two years.

PCM1 with cassette slot above the screen

In-Car Entertainment and Upgrades

The 996 was equipped with a range of stereo radios which were manufactured by Becker. These ranged from basic radio cassette players, to full satellite navigation systems and even included a Minidisk player. There were also options for CD-changers, amplifiers and cellular telephone systems. Most of these are getting rather outdated and some of the most popular forum questions are "how can I upgrade it", "how can I add an iPod" and "how do I integrate a Bluetooth phone". The answer to these questions can be complicated, depending on the equipment fitted and how important the "OEM Look" is to you.

Model numbers used here are for the RoW market. On 996.1 cars, US models usually have a '0' added to the CD or CDR model number.

When introduced in Europe for MY1998, 3 stereo units were offered, the CR11 and CR31 Radio-Cassette players and CDR21 Radio-CD player. All were offered in basic 4-speaker form (two dash and two rear), or with the M490 amplified 6-speaker system made by Harman (badged HAES) with the additional door speakers. Another option was the M680 Digital Sound Processing package – an equaliser located at the bottom of the centre console. The CDC-3 6-disk CD changer was also available.

MY1999 saw the model line-up change to the CR22 and CR32 Radio-Cassette, CDR22 Radio-CD, and MDR32 Minidisk player. More significant was the introduction of Porsche Communication Management PCM1, an integrated system of radio, cassette player and satellite navigation, with the options of a telephone and CD changer. The navigation unit was a separate CD drive made by Siemens, located directly under the double-height PCM unit. Again, the M490 and M680 options were available for each. The only significant change over the next 3 years was that the PCM navigation drive was updated from 8-bit to 16-bit on vehicles produced from 31st January 2001 onwards.

The same range continued into the MY2002 facelift with the replacement

PCM2 with CD slot above the screen and more buttons

CR21

MDR32 - closed

MDR32 - open

Becker GP

CDR23

of the DSP option with the M680 Bose analog amplifier.

MY2003 saw a significant change with the introduction of the MOST bus, short for Media Oriented System Transport. This is a fibre-optic ring, which passes sound and control signals between the head unit, amplifier, CD changer and telephone module. The CDR23 Radio-CD head unit was the standard audio head unit with an optional CDC4 CD-Changer. Two amplifier options were available, the M490 from Harman, and the M680 digital from Bose. PCM2 was the other major change for MY2003, when the CD navigation drive was incorporated into the main PCM unit.

Upgrades

So you can see that the upgrade possibilities are dependent on what system you have. The easiest to upgrade are the pre-MOST systems, as the wiring is generally compatible with aftermarket systems or with readily available adapter

cables. If you want to retain the OEM-look, then Becker produce more modern head units, such as the Grand Prix, TrafficPro, or Cascade, which have iPod and/or Bluetooth compatibility. At the time of writing these units are becoming less easily available, as Becker are now focussing

Pioneer AVIC double-DIN system fitted to my 996 Turbo

their production on the OEM market.

Alternatively, if you don't mind add-ons to your existing stereo, units such as the Solisto, Dension or Parrott may give you the functions you require at reasonable expense. Some of the CR and CDR models have an auxiliary input so simple connections for iPod can be made through these inputs, although the head unit cannot control the iPod, nor will it charge without a separate supply.

Double-DIN all-in-one aftermarket systems are an increasingly popular upgrade as all the functions of radio, CD, satellite navigation, Bluetooth, iPod and more are available. Units from manufacturers such as Pioneer, Alpine and Kenwood, for example, look very much at home in a 996 dash. Enlarging a single-slot head unit for double-DIN is relatively straightforward. The plastic frame containing the top two positions in the centre console can be modified to accept the cage of a dual height unit by removing the central plastic bar. The air conditioning controls can be moved to the lowest position in the console, as there is

plenty of cable in the loom to allow this. A new trim surround is required for the bottom position as it is a different shape, but this is very inexpensive.

Upgrading a MOST system is a very different prospect, because as far as I am aware there are no aftermarket units compatible with this technology. However, there are add-ons that can fully or partially integrate iPod and Bluetooth. Dension, MoBridge and NAV-TV manufacture such items. If you have PCM2 they can be controlled from the head unit, giving it the capability of more modern aftermarket systems. They are fairly expensive units, but the only real solution for integrating into an existing system. Replacing a MOST system with an aftermarket unit is also an expensive exercise.

The Harman and Bose MOST amplifiers have no inputs apart from the fibre-optic ones, so not only the head unit has to be replaced, but also the amplifier. To make matters worse, they use unusual loudspeaker impedances, so a speaker or wiring change is also on the cards.

Releases of map updates for PCM1 and

PCM2 have been sporadic in the past, but Porsche seem to have settled down to a more regular bi-annual period for the European market. On the early PCM1 systems with the 8-bit navigation drive, the only maps known to work are the genuine Porsche offering. For the 16-bit drive it has been found that maps for the Vauxhall/Opel Siemens NCDR/NCDC systems are compatible, provided a Porsche map of 2002-1 or later has been used on the system, which performs a software update.

Some owners set great store in keeping the car original so not to affect its saleability, but my view is that the majority of 996 models will never become collectible by virtue of the quantities made. It is less of an issue than it was on the early Porsche models. If you think a modern system is a good idea, there is a good chance that the next owner is likely to think the same way.

Problems

Pre MY2003 all radios and PCM had a user-entry security code. This was printed on a card and placed in the booklet wallet at delivery, but it is often lost or misplaced. If the battery is disconnected or goes flat, the code must be entered before the radio can be operated.

There are de-coding services (paid for) but the codes are stored on the Porsche IPAS system, so can be obtained from an OPC. Other organisations, such as RennTech.org have a de-coding service that can be obtained from the serial number of the radio.

Security codes are often stored in the DME Vehicle Data at the factory and can be read with a Porsche tester. Note that PCM1 has two codes – one for the PCM unit and one for the navigation module.

If your CD Changer stops working, the first thing to check is the fuse. On the side of the unit is a small cover, under which is a hidden fuse.

When the standard radio is replaced with an aftermarket unit there can be another common problem. Porsche radios have a security feature that grounds a wire to the alarm system when the radio is removed from the mounting cage, to activate the alarm. A common mistake is to attach this wire (brown & blue) directly to the cage, thereby grounding it. The result is that when the car is locked, the alarm horn gives a single beep. Remove the wire and insulate it.

Bose amplifiers on PCM2.0 up to MY2004 could suffer from sporadic sound failure. This can be remedied by an update to the amplifier using a special update CD inserted into the PCM unit.

First check your software version. To display this, press and hold the SET button, and press the AM-FM and AUDIO buttons at the same time. Scroll down and select 'SW Versions' with the right hand knob. If the amplifier software version shown is 00011927 (or lower) an update should be performed. The update CD is available from Porsche at a reasonable cost and is part number 000.043.205.50. Simply switch on the unit, insert the CD and the update will start automatically.

Occasionally, PCM2.0 units may freeze or lose functions. To reset the unit, press the 1, 4, and 8 buttons at the same time to force a system reboot. 996

Trackdays

Track Days are becoming increasingly popular as they are a great way to unleash the full potential and explore the limits of the car in controlled conditions. The first outing can be a bit daunting, but some simple basic preparation for both car and driver can help to reduce the anxiety.

Venue

There are many track day organisers, but it's important to choose one who work to defined standards for safety, organisation and regulation (in the UK look for an organiser who is a member of the Association of Track Day Organisers). Safety takes highest priority, but doesn't prevent you from enjoying your day any less.

Choose the venue for your first outing carefully. You can choose almost any circuit in the UK and find someone arranging track days there. Remember that no matter how good a driver you think you are, you are a novice on track. Talk to people with experience and ask for recommendations. Look at the circuit maps online. Choose one that isn't too complicated, is fairly level, has plenty of run-off area and not too many barriers. I would suggest that circuits like the Nürburgring are not the place to start!

It would be wise to look for a novice-only day, so that you are with like-minded people and don't feel intimidated by 'track day kings'.

Make sure the organisers have accredited (in the UK they might be ARDS (Association of Racing Driver Schools) instructors available for tuition sessions. It will help you enormously to have an instructor sitting in the passenger seat when you exit the pit lane for the first time. They can teach you the lines and braking points and keep a watchful eye on other cars until you get acclimatised.

Licence and Insurance

Quite understandably, you will need a valid full driver's licence and be required to show it on arrival.

Think about insurance. You can either take the sole risk yourself or get insurance cover. Your normal road policy will almost certainly not cover you for track days. Some insurers have add-on packages, so check your current insurer first. One-off day policies are also available, but check what is covered. Many only cover the damage to your car, not any third party. Track day collisions are very rare and most 'offs' are nobody's fault but the driver's.

Clothing

Are you appropriately dressed for the occasion? You won't be expected to have a full race suit with Nomex fireproof underwear and race boots, but you will need to dress correctly. Tighter fitting clothes with no bare flesh (arms and legs) exposed are the order of the day. Driving shoes and gloves are also a good idea. Whatever you wear, you need to be comfortable too. If it is a hot day, you can run the air conditioning to keep you cool, rather than stripping a layer of clothing or be buffeted by open windows.

You will certainly need a crash helmet. These can often be rented from the organisers on the day, but check

availability at the time of booking. If you think it might become a regular event for you and are considering buying one, bear in mind that it will need to conform to certain specifications. Requirements vary from country to country, but typical regulated safety standards include:

- BS6658 Type A/FR
- BS6658 Type A
- SNELL SA2005
- SNELL SA2000
- FIA 8860-2004
- SFI Foundation 31.1A, 31.2A

For further advice, consult the trackday organiser or motorsport authority.

Car Checks

So you know where you are going, the day is booked and you know what to wear. What should I do to the car?

Noise levels have become more stringently enforced in recent years. If you have a PSE (switchable exhaust), make sure it is working and will switch to quiet mode. If you have an aftermarket sports exhaust, make sure it meets the noise requirements. These vary from circuit to circuit and can also depend on the time of day. Some circuits also have 'noisy days' where there is no noise restriction, so if you have a loud exhaust you might want to find one of those.

The organiser will perform a static test, which is performed using a handheld sound meter. In the UK, each car is measured 0.5 metres (20 inches) away from the exhaust at a 45 degree angle, whilst the engine is being held at 75% of the maximum RPM. On 996s, this measurement will be taken at a point mid way between the two exhausts. In the UK, this level can be anywhere between 98 dB(A) and 105 dB(A). Some venues will also carry out drive-by tests during the day.

Check the condition of the tyres. They need to have enough tread on to complete the day and get you home safely and legally afterwards. Buy yourself a good quality tyre pressure gauge and set the pressures to the standard recommendation for your car

with cold tyres. Take the gauge with you and monitor the pressures throughout the day. Measure them as soon as you come in after each session. On the first session, the increased temperatures will elevate the pressures, so you will need to lower them to standard at that time. After subsequent sessions there should be less adjustment to be made. You may want to take a foot pump with you to add air if necessary or to get them back up to normal pressure for road use at the end of the day. With experience, you may also want to adjust pressures by a small amount to change the handling characteristics, but I would not recommend this on the first outing.

Get the wheel alignment checked. This should be done reasonably regularly anyway, but poor alignment will upset the car's handling and cause increased tyre wear. This will be emphasised even more on track.

Check the tightness of the wheel bolts, which should be 130Nm. If your wheels have been restored, paint can build up on the bolt seating cones and the wheel

bolts can work loose. Check them after each track session.

Check the brake discs/rotors and pads. Make sure the pads have at least 6-7mm of material left. You will find that the pads will wear at a much higher rate on track. If you decide to make track days a regular event, you might want to consider replacing them with a 'fast road' pad.

The brake fluid may need to be changed if it hasn't been recently. Brake fluid absorbs water and if not changed as in line with the service schedule this water can boil under heavy braking conditions and reduce braking force. Again, if you get enthusiastic, consider changing to a higher performance fluid, such as Castrol SRF, but also bear in mind that fluids such as this require more frequent changes.

Check the oil level, but don't be tempted to over-fill it 'just in case'. The oil will surge much more at track cornering speeds and overfilling can be detrimental. Filling to one or two bars below the maximum is probably the best level to

start the day, but do regular checks and perhaps take a 1 litre top-up bottle.

Another item you may want to consider is the CG-Lock for seat belts. This device fits to the standard seat belt and provides a locking mechanism for the lap section of the belt. It is highly effective at holding you tight in the seat, preventing you from sliding on the seat cushion.

Clean the windscreen and take some glass cleaner and cloths with you. The screen will build up with bugs and oil film, so clean it between sessions and at the end of the day.

Clean out the leaves and debris from the front inlet openings and check the condition of the radiators. Don't follow too closely behind other cars. Not only will you end up with stone chips on the front bumper, but flying stones and debris can damage the radiators. Take a small torch with you, so you can check them after each session. Keep an eye on the gauges when driving.

Remove all loose items from inside the car. Apart from being a distraction, it can be dangerous to have items floating around the cockpit. Empty the luggage compartment too. Find a cardboard box or plastic crate to fit all your bits and pieces in, such as foot pump, pressure gauge, screen cleaner, oil, drinks, and sandwiches, etc., so that you can lift it out when you get there and leave it in the pits. Make sure you have the towing eye with you, as some circuits insist on its fitting.

Fill the fuel tank before you arrive at the circuit. The fuel consumption will be at least twice that of normal driving and if your car runs out of fuel on track it will be towed to a safe position and may be left there for the rest of the day. The organisers will let you know where the nearest filling stations are, should you need to top up during the day.

Personal Preparation

It might sound over-the-top, but prepare yourself mentally. Study the circuit map carefully. Visualise driving the circuit. Know which bends are coming up and where you are in the lap. Note the pit entrance and exit points. Look on YouTube, as there may well be some in-car video from the circuit for you to study. Computer games also have many of the major circuits on them and are a good source of practice. Even F1 drivers use them!

Learn the flag system. You will get detailed advice at the driver's briefing but general usage for track days is usually limited to the main 6 flags:

● **Yellow** – Caution, incident ahead
● **Red** – Session stopped, slow to a crawl and return to the pits
● **Red and Yellow stripes** – Slippery conditions, usually oil on the track
● **Blue** – faster car behind wishes to overtake
● **Black** – Return to pits, car problem or bad behaviour
● **Chequered Flag** – End of session

No doubt that on the first time out onto the circuit your heart will be pounding and the adrenaline flowing. Remain calm and focussed in this situation, breathing steadily and smoothly.

On the day

You will get detailed instructions from the organisers prior to the event, but a typical beginner's track day would have the following format:

Signing On: The organisers will check your driving licence, ask you to sign indemnity forms and assign you an instructor if you booked one.

Noise Test and safety checks: Your car will need to pass the noise test as outlined above before you are allowed on track. They will also check safety features such as seat belt condition and operation.

Driver's Briefing: This is a group session and all safety aspects will be covered. It will cover everything you need to know, such as rules for overtaking, flags and driving techniques. Listen carefully! Some circuits also carry out on-circuit briefing, where they will take you on the circuit in a minibus driven by an instructor to show you details of each corner.

Familiarisation Laps: Some circuits also carry out familiarisation laps, where drivers follow a 'pace car' at reduced speed to show the racing lines.

Track Time: The track day begins. Take it steady to start with, warm up your engine and tyres and build your speed gradually throughout the day. Keep a good eye on the rear view mirrors as much as possible. There will be much faster cars and drivers out there and you may not be driving as they expect. Be aware and give them a wide berth to avoid a collision.

Additional Briefings: There are often short briefing sessions throughout the day, to help you improve your technique as the day goes on.

At the end of a session

When the session ends, slow down and try not to use the brakes on the slowing down lap. This will give them a chance to cool. Slow right down in the pit entrance road and watch the speedometer. You will be going faster than you think. Leave the engine idling for a few minutes if possible, especially if you have a Turbo, to give the engine a chance to cool down more gradually. Don't apply the handbrake until the brakes are fully cooled – just leave it in gear. Check the tyre pressures, front radiators, oil and brake fluid levels and get yourself a drink of water. You have earned it!

And lastly.........

Track Days are strictly non-competitive, so don't go with the attitude that you are going to set the place alight. Also, timing devices are not allowed, nor is any form of racing. You are there to explore the limits of the car, but more importantly the limits of your ability. Go beyond either and it will end in tears!

Don't be upset if other cars go blasting past you. You aren't trying to prove anything and who knows what greater circuit experience, engine power or special tyres they have.

Enjoy your day, make friends and come away with the satisfying feeling of getting the first event under your belt. As you leave the circuit, watch your speed and adjust your driving style back to 'street mode'. 996

Richard Hamilton

Richard Hamilton started his working life in the new engine design department of Petters Diesels in the mid '70s. From there he moved to Sir WG Armstrong Whitworth & Co working on the design of military and research engines, primarily, opposed-piston two-stroke diesels. Many were used in vehicles such as the Chieftain and Challenger battle tanks and the BAE Rapier missile launcher.

In the mid '80s he joined his family business, TW Hamilton Design Ltd, which designs and manufactures specialist seed sowing machinery for the horticultural industry.

After racing karts as a junior, he has always been a keen motoring enthusiast and technophile. More recently he was involved with the diagnostics and datalogging for a 996 Cup car in the Britcar endurance series in the UK.

Acknowledgements

I would like to acknowledge some of the many people who assisted with the material and freely gave their assistance in the writing of this book. Thanks must first go to my good friend Tony Wright of Wrightune (www.wrightune.co.uk) in Oxfordshire, UK, who got me started in the delights of Porsche ownership and with his assistant, Joe Carter, assisted with many of the do-it-yourself sections described in this book.

Thanks also go to all my friends and fellow members of Porsche Club GB, notably Min Chew, Rod Naghar, Barry Smith and Andy Watling. Other invaluable sources of information were provided by Loren Cook and members of RennTech (www.renntech.org).

Club membership, in particular my involvement with the forum (www.porscheclubgbforum.com), has been a particularly enjoyable part of the ownership experience to me and is a great resource for information and to share knowledge. If you have a desire to learn more about these marvellous machines, forums are fantastic sources.

My final and most sincere thanks must go to my long-suffering wife Julie, for putting up with me and allowing me to indulge in my passion. For that, I will be ever grateful. *996*

Index